English for Journalists

Third edition

Wynford Hicks

 Routledge
Taylor & Francis Group

LONDON AND NEW YORK

First published 1993
by Routledge
2 Park Square, Milton Park, Abingdon, Oxon OX14 4RN

Simultaneously published in the USA and Canada
by Routledge
270 Madison Ave, New York, NY 10016

Reprinted 1995, 1996, 1997

Second edition 1998
Reprinted 1999 (twice), 2000 (twice), 2001, 2003 (twice), 2004, 2005, 2007

Third edition 2007

Routledge is an imprint of the Taylor & Francis Group, an informa business

© 1993, 1998, 2007 Wynford Hicks

Typeset in Goudy and Scala Sans by
Florence Production Ltd, Stoodleigh, Devon
Printed and bound in Great Britain by
TJ International Ltd, Padstow, Cornwall

British Library Cataloguing in Publication Data
A catalogue record for this book is available from the British Library

Library of Congress Cataloging in Publication Data
A catalog record for this book has been requested

ISBN10: 0–415–40419–3 (hbk)
ISBN10: 0–415–40420–7 (pbk)
ISBN10: 0–203–96766–6 (ebk)

ISBN13: 978–0–415–40419–8 (hbk)
ISBN13: 978–0–415–40420–4 (pbk)
ISBN13: 978–0–203–96766–9 (ebk)

Contents

Author's note

English for Journalists is now part of the Media Skills series. Other titles develop points made here in greater detail. For example, *Writing for Journalists* includes a fuller treatment of style and *Subediting for Journalists* a chapter on house style.

There is no chapter on broadcast journalism in this edition of *English for Journalists*. There did not seem to be a need to include one now that the Media Skills series includes books on broadcast journalism. However, many of the points made here apply as much to broadcast journalism as to print.

Wynford Hicks
wynford@hicksinfrance.net

1
The state of English

Since the second edition of *English for Journalists* was published in 1998 there has been more public discussion about the state of the language than ever before. Newspaper and magazine articles, TV and radio programmes, website messages and individual emails pour forth an endless stream of information, comment and jokes about English.

Some newspapers now publish editions of their style guides on their websites as well as in book form. The *Guardian* has also published several highly entertaining collections of its corrected mistakes, particularly of English usage, with commentary by its readers' editor.

After the runaway success of *Eats, Shoots & Leaves* by Lynne Truss, many bookshops established a separate section for language guides and commentaries. Now there's no aspect of English too obscure to have a book devoted to it. Next to the dictionaries, usage handbooks and alphabetical lists of difficult words, there are anthologies of such things as clichés, rhyming slang, modern slang, insulting quotations, euphemisms, language myths . . . Anybody looking for entertainment and enlightenment in the English language must surely find it.

But lively debate and spectacular book sales do not add up to a dramatic improvement in national writing ability. Take British university students, for example. The fact is that most of them lack the basic writing skills. This is the shocking but clear message of a report called *Writing Matters* published by the Royal Literary Fund in March 2006. It is based on the experience of 130 writers who worked as RLF fellows in 71 universities, offering students tuition in how to write a letter or an essay, how to draft a report or draw up a job application.

A similar – but wider – message was delivered in March 2003 by Bloomsbury, the publisher of the Encarta Concise Dictionary, who consulted 42 professors or teachers of English in Britain, the US, Canada and Australia. They reported strikingly similar problems among students in the four countries.

The RLF report emphasises that the problems apply across the whole range of ability – 'from students aiming for a first to those struggling to avoid a fail' – and afflict those on arts courses as well as scientists. 'What is worrying,' one fellow reported of three particular students, 'is that these young people are students of English literature at an "elite" university. They ought to have attained, by this stage, a reasonably high level of written proficiency but . . . they have genuine difficulty in writing a basic English sentence.'

Summarising the report's findings in an article in the *Sunday Times*, the biographer Hilary Spurling writes: 'The students' essays are muddled and clumsily expressed. They don't know where to start, how to organise their subject matter or follow a coherent chain of thought. They suffer, as another fellow succinctly put it, from lexical nullity and syntactical bankruptcy – their stuff is unreadable, and sometimes unintelligible as well.

> Meagre vocabulary, slack phrasing, tortured syntax, incompetent punctuation: these . . . mean that teachers in higher education . . . spend an increasing amount of their time correcting grammar, spelling and punctuation, and trying to explain how an essay is meant to be structured.

So who and what are to blame? 'Part of the trouble,' Spurling says, 'is that, until they reach university, most young people have never felt any need to write. They belong to a tick-box culture based on speeded-up electronic responses in education as in other fields.' Elsewhere in the *Sunday Times* the columnist Minette Marrin includes ticking boxes as one of a number of educational evils, pointing the finger of blame for students' poor writing skills:

> at bad schools, at bad teaching, at the shortage of able teachers now that able women have many other opportunities besides teaching, at failed methods of teaching reading, at child-centred learning and other disastrous educational orthodoxies, at the abandonment of grammar and learning by heart, at the distractions of computers, at tick-boxes and coursework, which encourage laziness and internet plagiarism.

To which could be added, surely, the bad example provided by much of the media. Just as journalism students are not immune from the general weakness in writing, so the practice of a newspaper like the *Sunday Times* can be said to be part of the problem. Mistakes of grammar, spelling and punctuation, peculiar vocabulary and clumsy constructions undermine attempts made elsewhere to raise standards – and certainly reduce the impact of those why-oh-why columns on students' terrible English.

How about this from the edition of the *Sunday Times* (26 March 2006) that reported on *Writing Matters*?

> I'm a great fan of the chef, John Williams, who once graced Claridge's. Which has been semi-desecrated. Although I dropped in recently and their Gordon Ramsay restaurant was very busy.

This is so bad it's stretching a point to call it writing at all. What was that about 'a basic English sentence'?

There's no attempt at construction here. The writer, Michael Winner, just plonks his thoughts down as they occur to him. And he keeps on doing it, scattering full stops like confetti:

> I've lost two and a half stone. I decline to use kilograms. Foreign muck. The vegetables were perfect. Even though they didn't have fresh peas.

The failure to write coherently in sentences is one of the most common faults in modern journalism. Another is the perverse use of language: how can Claridge's be 'semi-desecrated'? Either something is desecrated or it isn't. Yet another common fault is grammatical confusion between singular and plural. Describing Claridge's, Winner lurches from the singular ('*has* been semi-desecrated') to the plural ('and *their* Gordon Ramsay restaurant').

As well as mismatches of singular and plural, the *Sunday Times* of 26 March 2006 includes several dangling modifiers, such as this one in a reader's letter:

> Several years ago, while on a sightseeing pony and trap around New Orleans, the driver pointed out a large building which he told us was the House of the Rising Sun.

Is the driver sightseeing? No, it's the reader. And in the next example (from a political gossip column) money can't be 'like marriages':

> Like most rocky marriages, money is the problem.

Journalistic writing is increasingly informal, colloquial and so has a tendency to become ungrammatical. Here's another example of bad grammar (from a different gossip column):

> It is sad when streets − with the possible exception of Hogarth's Gin Lane − lose old associations; but as us scruffs learnt leaving Fleet Street, it can be a liberation . . .

'Us scruffs' is wrong, ugly and, I think, pretentious. Are we scruffs trying to pretend we're proles not toffs? Anyway what's an expression like this doing in an edition of the *Sunday Times* that preaches the need to write well?

By contrast with what we might call the Michael Winner school of journalism, there are stylish writers who occasionally lapse. Simon Jenkins, a past editor of the *Times* and the London *Evening Standard*, has a column and a book review in the *Sunday Times* of 26 March 2006. In the column, about Tony Blair's foreign policy, he writes:

> Blair's attempt to bond Al-Qaeda, Saddam Hussein, Iran's mullahs, the Taliban and Hamas into some giant global conspiracy is both inaccurate and distorts coherent strategy.

The problem here is that with the emphatic expression 'both . . . and . . .' the two phrases that follow must be grammatically equivalent, so to be correct, you would need something like:

> Blair's attempt . . . is both inaccurate and a distortion of coherent strategy./Blair's attempt . . . both is inaccurate and distorts coherent strategy.

The first alternative replaces a verb by a noun (usually a bad idea); the second sounds clumsy. There's a third option: lose the 'both' altogether.

The Jenkins book review includes a mistake that is increasingly common in words taken from French (other examples are émigré and pâté): 'résumé' meaning summary appears with only one of its accents as 'resumé', which is not a word in any language. (To show how difficult it is to get this right, the published version of the *Guardian* style book prescribes rather than proscribes 'resumé', though the error has been corrected in the website version.)

Hyphens are another problem area. While some writers omit essential ones, others put them in where they have no possible function, after an '-ly' adverb, as in:

> Bennett was poached from the Canberra Raiders to be appointed the first coach of the newly-formed Brisbane Broncos in 1988 . . .

But the *Sunday Times* writer responsible for the redundant hyphen is in prestigious company. The 2003 edition of the Collins English Dictionary includes an unnecessary hyphen after an '-ly' adverb in its entry for 'pharming', which is quoted on the dust jacket:

> the practice of rearing or growing genetically-modified animals or plants in order to develop pharmaceutical products.

This is clearly a mistake rather than conscious policy for elsewhere in Collins, in the entry for 'genetically modified' for example, there are no hyphens; the example given is *genetically modified food*.

These are symptoms of a general malaise in publishing: book reviewers often complain about poor standards of editing and proofreading. But then there are those who say, about the state of English, 'Crisis? What crisis?' and attack the whole notion of correctness. The radicals, who tend to be academics in university departments of linguistics, say that standard English is only one dialect among many and should not necessarily be preferred to the others (for a fuller account of their position, see the introduction to my book *Quite Literally*). Their influence on public policy and the teaching of English – via the colleges of education where their views have been dominant – has been profound, extensive and malign.

But the popularity of *Eats, Shoots & Leaves* has undermined their position – and they seem to be aware of it. In a recent book called *How Language Works* David Crystal, a former professor of linguistics at Reading University, launches a wild attack on the presumption of prescriptive conservatives like Lynne Truss:

Believing in the inviolability of the small set of rules that they have managed themselves to acquire, they condemn others from a different dialect background, or who have not had the same educational opportunities as themselves, for not following those same rules. Enthused by the Stalinesque policing metaphor, they advocate a policy of zero tolerance, to eradicate all traces of the aberrant behaviour. This extreme attitude would be condemned by most people if it were encountered in relation to such domains as gender or race, but for some reason it is tolerated in relation to language. Welcomed, even, judging by the phenomenal sales of *Eats, Shoots & Leaves*.

This is strong stuff from academe. Admittedly, the phrase 'zero tolerance' itself is pretty strong – and it does appear in the subtitle to Truss's book. But in fact her tone is more wry and whimsical than 'Stalinesque', which is one of the reasons why she has been so successful. Early on, she claims that she is not setting out to instruct about punctuation – 'there are already umpteen excellent punctuation guides on the market' – and she often expresses doubt, even confusion, on particular points.

For example, she says that 'one shouldn't be too rigid about the Oxford comma' (sometimes it's a good idea; sometimes not). She concedes that hyphen usage is 'just a big bloody mess and is likely to get messier'. And on whether the possessive of names ending in 's' should have a second 's' (Truss' or Truss's), she says: 'There are no absolute rights and wrongs in this matter.'

She even says that St Thomas's Hospital in south London can make up its own mind whether it wants people to add the extra 's' or not. Well, no, I don't think it can: here Truss is being too tolerant. The sound argument (in every sense) is that where the extra 's' is sounded in speech, it should be included in writing. Because we say 'St *Thomas's*', I think we should write it.

But of course she is quite right to point out that the experts disagree on aspects of usage, particularly punctuation and grammar. Also, some words can be correctly spelt (or should that be spelled?) in more than one way and others create a problem because they mean different things to different people. This strengthens the argument for newspapers and magazines to decide on a house style to avoid irritating inconsistency.

House style can include everything from minor detail – whether to use single quotes or double, when to use italics – to major policy on things like four-letter words and political correctness. Published and internet style books also provide a very useful commentary on changing English usage.

For example, both the *Times* (online) and the *Economist* (published book) disagree with the *Guardian* (online and published) on accents. They both say we should keep accents, eg on café, cliché and communiqué, when they make a crucial difference to pronunciation.

The *Times* is pretty prescriptive about none, which 'almost always takes the singular verb', while the *Economist* is more relaxed: none 'usually takes a singular verb'. But the *Guardian*, which used to insist on it, now says: 'It is a (very persistent) myth that "none" has to take a singular verb.'

By contrast, on 'like' and 'such as', it is the *Economist* that now takes the liberal position. Whereas the *Guardian* and the *Times* still disapprove, the *Economist* bites the bullet: 'Authorities like Fowler and Gowers is an acceptable alternative to authorities such as Fowler and Gowers.'

I agree with the liberal view on both points. The entry on 'like' and 'such as ' has been changed in this edition of *English for Journalists*, as have the entries on 'hopefully', 'that' and 'which' and several others. A new entry, 'One word not two', includes examples like 'subeditor' and 'underway' and there are numerous additions and amendments.

The biggest change in this edition is to include many more examples of published mistakes to illustrate the points made. The general policy remains what it has always been: to promote a standard, but not stuffy, English.

2
Grammar: the rules

Grammar is the set of rules and conventions that are the basis of the language.

Early English grammars were derived from the rules of Latin. The result was that they were over-rigid and even included 'rules' that did not apply to English at all. For example, there is no rule of English grammar that prohibits split infinitives, or prepositions to end sentences, or conjunctions to start them. These are matters of style not grammar.

In the 1960s English grammar was accused of restricting the personal development and free expression of young people. The previously accepted form of standard English was declared to be both a straitjacket on self-expression and a devious means of keeping the working class and ethnic minorities in their place. The result was that in many politically correct classrooms the teaching of English grammar was virtually abandoned.

But the pendulum has swung back, and learning the rules of grammar is now an important part of the national curriculum. This is surely right – above all, for journalists, who act as interpreters between the sources they use and their readers and listeners. Not to know the grammar of their own language is a big disadvantage for a writer – and a crippling one for a subeditor.

A comprehensive English grammar would constitute a book of its own. What follows is an attempt to list the main grammatical terms and rules you need to know.

Note: the term 'syntax', meaning grammatical structure in sentences, is not used in this book. Instead the general term 'grammar' is used to cover both the parts of speech and the structure of sentences.

The parts of speech

Traditionally, there are eight parts of speech: noun, pronoun, adjective, verb, adverb, preposition, conjunction and interjection, with the article ('a/an' or 'the') now often added to the list instead of being considered an adjective. There are various possible subdivisions: verbs can be 'auxiliary'; pronouns can be 'demonstrative' and 'possessive'. Numerals can be included as a separate category.

Article

'The' is the definite article; 'a' or 'an' is the indefinite article. 'An' replaces 'a' before a vowel (an owl), unless the vowel is sounded as a consonant (a use), and before a silent h (an hour).

Noun

Nouns are the names of people and things. They are either ordinary nouns called *common* (thing, chair) or special nouns called *proper* ('George', 'Tuesday'). Proper nouns often take a capital letter.

Abstract common nouns refer to qualities ('beauty', 'honesty'), emotions ('anger', 'pity') or states ('friendship', 'childhood').

In general nouns are *singular* ('thing', 'man') or *plural* ('things', 'men'). But some nouns are the same in the singular and the plural ('aircraft', 'sheep') and some are used only in the plural ('scissors', 'trousers'). Nouns that refer to collections of people and things ('the cabinet', 'the team') are known as *collective* nouns.

Pronoun

Pronouns stand for nouns and are often used to avoid repetition. They can be:

> *personal* (**I, you, him**)
> *possessive* (**mine, yours, his**)
> *reflexive/intensive* (**myself, yourself, himself**)

relative/interrogative (**who, whose, whom**)
indefinite (**anybody, none, each**)
demonstrative (**this, that, these** and **those** are the four demonstrative pronouns)

The noun that a pronoun stands for is called its *antecedent*.

Pronouns, unlike nouns, often change their form according to the role they play in a sentence: 'I' becomes 'me'; 'you' becomes 'yours'. This role of a noun or pronoun is called *case*. Following the Latin model, grammarians used to talk about such things as the nominative, dative and genitive cases. But this is needlessly complicated: the key distinction is between the *subjective* case ('I') and the *objective* case ('me').

Verb

Verbs express action or a state of being or becoming ('doing word' is therefore an over-simplification). They can be *finite* because they have a subject ('he thinks') or *non-finite* because they do not ('to think'). The *tense* of a verb shows whether it refers to the past, the present or the future. Tenses are formed in two ways: either by inflecting (changing the form of) the verb ('he *thought*') or by adding an auxiliary verb ('he *will* think') or both ('he *has thought*'). Verbs can be *active* ('he thinks') or *passive* ('it was thought').

Finite verbs

Mood: finite verbs can be

> *indicative,* either statement ('he thinks') or question ('does he think?')
> *conditional* ('I would think')
> *subjunctive* ('if he were to think')
> *imperative* ('go on, think!')

Indicative tenses

There are three basic times (present, past, future) and three basic actions (simple, continuing, completed). Thus there are nine basic tenses:

	Simple	Continuing	Completed
Present	I see	I am seeing	I have seen
Past	I saw	I was seeing	I had seen
Future	I will see	I will be seeing	I will have seen

Three other tenses show a mixture of continuing and completed action:

Present: I have been seeing
Past: I had been seeing
Future: I will have been seeing

Traditional grammar distinguishes between the first person singular ('I'), the second person singular ('thou'), the third person singular ('he/she'), the first person plural ('we'), the second person plural ('you') and the third person plural ('they'). But modern English has dispensed with the second person singular ('thou' is archaic), and in most verbs only the third person singular differs from the standard form:

I see
He/she sees
We see
You see
They see

In both future and conditional tenses 'will'/'would' is now the standard form, except in certain questions. In the past, it was considered correct to use 'shall' after I/we for the plain future ('We shall be late') while 'will' was reserved for emphasis ('We *will* catch this train'); and 'will' after he/she/you/they ('He will be late') while 'shall' was reserved for emphasis ('He *shall* catch this train'). An example of this is the English version of Marshal Pétain's first world war slogan *They shall not pass* (revived by the Republicans in the Spanish civil war).

'Shall' is still used after I/we in questions that make some kind of offer or suggestion ('Shall I phone for a taxi?'), though not in straightforward ones that ask for information ('Will we get a drink at the press launch?').

Conditional tenses
There are two conditional tenses, the present and the past, both formed by the addition of would ('I would think', 'I would have thought').

Subjunctive tenses
The verb forms for the subjunctive mood are much the same as for the indicative. But there are two exceptions.

The third person singular, present tense, changes as follows:

> 'She *has* faith' becomes 'If she *have* faith'
>
> 'He *finds*' becomes 'Should he *find*'.

The verb 'to be' changes as follows:

Present

Indicative	Subjunctive (if)
I am	I be
He/she is	He/she be
We are	We be
You are	You be
They are	They be

Past

Indicative	Subjunctive (if)
I was	I were
He/she was	He/she were

'We were', 'you were' and 'they were' remain unchanged.

Non-finite verbs

There are three types of non-finite verb:

1 the *infinitive* (**see/to see**)
2 the *present participle* or *gerund* (**seeing**)
3 the *past participle* (**seen**)

The infinitive usually, but not always, has 'to' before it. 'I want *to see*' and 'I can't *see*' are both examples of the infinitive.

The participles are used to make up the basic tenses (see above).

The participles are also used as adjectives ('a far-seeing statesman', 'an unseen passage') and in phrases ('seeing him in the street, I stopped for a chat'). Here, although the subject of 'seeing' is not stated, it is implied: the person doing the seeing is 'I'.

The gerund has the same -ing form as the present participle but is a verb-noun ('seeing is believing').

Adjective

An adjective describes a noun or pronoun.

Demonstrative adjectives ('this', 'that', 'these', 'those') identify a noun ('this car', 'these potatoes'). When used without a noun they become pronouns ('this is my car').

Possessive adjectives ('my', 'your', 'our') show ownership ('my car').

Most other adjectives are *absolute adjectives* ('final', 'perfect') or *adjectives of degree*.

Adjectives of degree are either

> *positive*, used of a thing ('hot', 'complicated')
> *comparative*, used to compare one thing with another ('hotter', 'more complicated')
> *superlative*, used to compare a thing with two or more others ('hottest', 'most complicated')

Adverb

An adverb usually describes a verb, adjective or other adverb:

> He sees *clearly* [adverb describes verb].
>
> It was a *newly* minted coin [adverb describes adjective].
>
> He sees *very* clearly [adverb describes adverb].

Some adverbs are used to link sentences; they are called *sentence adverbs* or *conjunctive adverbs* and are usually marked off by commas:

> Life is expensive. Death, *however,* is cheap.

Note that 'however' can also be used as an ordinary adverb:

> *However* good you may be at punctuation, you will still make mistakes.

Preposition

A preposition is a word that links its object with a preceding word or phrase:

It's a case *of* mumps.

We're going *to* Blackpool.

When the object of a preposition is a pronoun it must be in the objective case. Thus:

of me
to her
for him
by us
with them

Conjunction

A conjunction is a word that:

1   links two similar parts of speech

fit *and* well
slowly *but* surely

2   links two sentences whether or not they are separated by a full stop

You may come. *Or* you may go.
You may come *or* you may go.

3   links main clauses with subordinate clauses and phrases

I will *if* you will.
I will go *as* a clown.

Interjection

An interjection is a short exclamation that is outside the main sentence. It either stands alone or is linked to the sentence by a comma:

Alas! Woe is me!

Hello, how are you?

Sentences

A sentence is traditionally described as a group of words expressing a complete thought. It has a *subject*, the person or thing being discussed, and a *verb*, expressing action or a state of being (and it may have other elements such as an object):

Subject	verb
The man	sees.

Sometimes the subject is understood rather than stated:

The old man lay down. And died.

In the second sentence 'he' is understood.

There is also a looser definition of a sentence:

> ... a piece of writing or speech between two full stops or equivalent pauses
> (*New Shorter Oxford English Dictionary*, 1993)

Sadly, this attempted catch-all fails to include the *first* sentence in a piece.

But a single word can certainly be a sentence:

Agreed.
Indeed.

The first of these consists of a verb with the subject implied; the second can mean the same thing. In each case what makes the word a sentence is that it expresses a complete thought. So the definition we started with holds – with two minor revisions:

A sentence is *a word or group of words* expressing a complete thought and ending with a full stop.

Transitive verbs and objects

A sentence may have an *object*, the person or thing that receives the action of the verb. This kind of verb is called *transitive*:

Subject	verb	object
The man	sees	the sun.

An object may be *direct* or *indirect*:

Subject	verb	direct object	indirect object
The man	gives	the dog	to his son.

Subject	verb	indirect object	direct object
The man	gives	the dog	a bone.

'To' is sometimes, but not always, included with an indirect object.

Intransitive verbs

If nothing receives the action of the verb it is *intransitive*:

Subject	verb
The man	walks.

Intransitive verbs are often followed by something to extend their meaning but this is not called an object:

The man walks slowly [adverb].
The man walks to work [adverbial phrase].

Active and passive verbs

A transitive verb is in the *active voice*. It can also be turned round so that it is in the *passive voice*:

Active
The man sees the sun.

Passive
The sun is seen by the man.

Be careful when you combine the passive with a participle:

> The workers were penalised by sending them back.

is incorrect because the subject of both main verb (stated) and participle (implied) must be the same. Instead write either:

> They penalised the workers by sending them back.

or:

> The workers were penalised by being sent back.

Inactive verbs and complements

If a verb expresses not action but a state of being it is inactive and takes a *complement*.

Subject	*verb*	*complement*
The man	is	ill.
He	feels	a fool.

Some verbs can be either transitive or inactive:

> He feels ill [complement].
>
> He feels the cloth [object].

Whereas both direct and indirect objects are in the objective case, complements, like their subjects, are traditionally in the subjective case:

> I see him [object].
>
> I am he [complement].

But the common form 'It's me' (rather than 'It is I') is now accepted by almost everybody.

Agreement of the verb

The verb must agree with its subject in person and number:

> I give.

but:

> He gives [person].
>
> Spelling is important.

but:

> Spelling and grammar are important [number].

1   Note that words joined to a single subject by a preposition do not affect the verb:

> Spelling, with grammar, is important.

2   If two subjects are linked by 'either, or' or 'neither, nor' the verb agrees with the nearer subject:

> Neither the news editor nor any of his reporters have received the call.

3   If one subject is affirmative and the other negative the verb agrees with the affirmative one:

> The chief sub, not her deputies, was at lunch.

4   The verb in a defining clause agrees with its nearer antecedent:

> He was one of the best subs that have ever worked here.

5   Nouns that are plural in form but singular in meaning take a singular verb:

> News is what the reader wants to know.
>
> Thirty pages is a lot of copy.
>
> Law and order was a plus for New Labour.

In the last example 'law and order' takes a singular verb because it is a routine combination. If we separate the two elements we need a plural verb:

> 'Law' and 'order' are both nouns.

6   The word 'number' is treated as singular when it is a figure but as plural when it means 'a few':

> A number is stamped on each computer.

but:

> A number of computers are needed.

7   Singular pronouns such as 'everyone' take a singular verb. 'None' can be either singular or plural:

> Are there any bananas? No, there are none.
>
> Is there any beer? No, there is none.

8   Collective nouns take either a singular or a plural verb according to sense:

> The team is small [it has few players].

but:

> The team are small [its players are not big].
>
> The cabinet is determined [it is seen as a single body].

but:

> The cabinet are discussing [it takes at least two to discuss].
>
> The cabinet is divided [it must be seen as one before it can be divided].

but:

> The cabinet are agreed [it takes more than one to agree].

Do not mix the two forms. Do not write:

> The cabinet is divided but they are discussing . . .

Many house-style books insist on organisations being treated as singular.

Sentence structure

A sentence with only one verb is a *simple* sentence:

> The man sees the sun.

A sentence with two or more main verbs is a *compound* sentence:

> The man sees the sun and he closes his eyes.

A sentence with one or more main verbs and one or more subsidiary verbs is a *complex* sentence:

> The man who sees the sun closes his eyes.

Clauses

A clause is a group of words including a subject and a verb forming part of a sentence. A compound sentence has two or more main clauses; a complex sentence has at least one main clause and at least one subordinate clause. In the previous example, the main clause is 'The man closes his eyes' and the subordinate clause is 'who sees the sun'.

There is an important distinction between clauses that define and those that do not. Commas help to make this distinction clear:

> The man who sees the sun closes his eyes
> [in general a man who sees the sun will close his eyes].
>
> The man, who sees the sun, closes his eyes
> [this particular man, having seen the sun, closes his eyes].

According to traditional grammar 'that' should be used in defining clauses referring to things:

> This is the house that Jack built
> [clause defines the house].

Whereas 'which' should be used in non-defining clauses:

> Fred's house, which was built in 1937, is up for sale
> [clause does not restrict, adds incidental information].

With people, on the other hand, either 'that' or 'who'/'whom' is used to define:

> This is the man that/who sold them the house.

Whereas 'who'/'whom' must be used in non-defining clauses since 'which' is not used of people:

> Fred, who was born in 1937, sold them the house.

'Which' is increasingly accepted, at least in Britain, as an alternative to 'that' for defining clauses:

> This is the house which Fred bought.

But 'that' should never be used for non-defining clauses. Avoid:

Fred's house, that was built in 1937, is up for sale.

Phrases

A phrase is a group of words without a verb forming part of a sentence. An adjectival phrase must be related to the correct noun or pronoun.

A readable book, it has a good index.

Correct: the phrase 'a readable book' describes the subject 'it'.

A readable book, its value is enhanced by a good index.

Incorrect: the phrase 'a readable book' cannot describe the subject 'its value'.

Like Belfast, Beirut has known civil war.

Correct: the phrase 'like Belfast' describes the subject 'Beirut'.

Unlike Belfast, bomb blasts no longer echo across the city.

Incorrect: the phrase 'unlike Belfast' cannot describe the subject 'bomb blasts'.

This mistake is called the dangling modifier. A particularly common example of it is the dangling, floating or hanging participle:

Walking across the road, he was run over by a car.

Correct: the phrase 'walking across the road' describes the subject 'he'.

Walking across the road, a car ran him over.

Incorrect: the phrase 'walking across the road' cannot describe the subject 'a car'.

3
Grammar: 10 common mistakes

Here are some examples of the most common mistakes made in journalism.

1 The dangling modifier

A renowned and stylish beauty, her photograph appeared in magazines throughout the world. (obituary)

Literally a room for wine, the cobblestone city is littered with these convivial boltholes. (travel caption)

The composer of Lord of the Dance, his life was a musical journey in search of an unconventional God. (obit heading)

But the beauty isn't the photograph; the room isn't the city; the composer isn't the life.

Like many vicarage children life was peripatetic. (diary)

Like lots of his contemporaries, Kerouac and Burroughs were on his bookshelves. (feature)

There is usually something lingering about a Catholic formation even if, like James Joyce, it later turns to passionate hostility. (feature)

No, life is not like children and a Catholic formation is not like Joyce. In the second example readers might be misled into thinking he had 'lots of his contemporaries' on his bookshelves.

The floating participle (a particular case of the dangling modifier)

If participles float, identity may be mistaken:

> After nearly burning down the house by leaving an empty pot on the stove, the sisters arranged for a neighbour to bring Ruth her dinner every evening. (feature)

But it was Ruth, not the sisters, who nearly burnt the house down.

> Not long afterwards, having returned from a hunting trip to nearby Donegal, an IRA unit tried to sledgehammer their way through the front door of their home. (feature)

But it wasn't the IRA who went on the hunting trip.

> After making his debut in the Millennium Stadium defeat, Williams watched the hooker play for Glasgow and phoned him to say that the scrum was not good enough. (feature)

But Williams was the coach: it was the hooker who made his debut at the Millennium Stadium.

> 'I know this makes me sound like a security guard,' he explained. 'But having tried to defend her interests in the past, she says she'd be happier with me present.' (feature)

But it was he, not she, who had tried to defend her interests in the past.

'Born', in features and obituaries, is a warning sign – it rarely means what it says:

> Born in Singapore, her Singaporean-Chinese mother divorced her father . . . when she was three. (feature)

> Born Bettye, in Peoria, her mother had edited a local newspaper's women's page before becoming a housewife. (obit)

Then there are the amusing ones – purchases that pop out, books that write etc:

> Popping out to the local sandwich shop last week, their purchases were handed to them in sponsored bags. (feature)

As well as writing about obelisks, mummies, papyrus and Chinese ideograms, his books dealt with codes and code-breaking . . . (book review)

But having won that battle decisively, the ground has dramatically shifted. (column)

Buried deep in Queensland, Australia, her experiences as Connery's wife seem a million miles away. Having wed at the fresh-faced start of their careers, their marriage quickly dissolved into one long, mistrustful squabble. (feature)

2 Number disagreement

2a Verb clash

Half work in the media and the other half is waiting to perform. (feature)

It's not often that the international press takes an interest in our politics, but they are now. (column)

2b Noun/pronoun clash

The decline of the grey nurse shark is exacerbated by the fact that it takes them up to 10 years to reach full maturity. (picture caption)

2c Pronoun clash

They are the only major party to have increased its vote over the past eight years . . . (feature)

2d Pronoun/verb clash

To celebrate the 10th anniversary of their Dover-Calais route, SeaFrance Ferries has created 10 special Easter breaks . . . (news story)

Of course the Bangladesh team clings to their Test status eagerly. (feature)

The jury is still considering their verdicts in the case of White . . .
(news story)

The top brass at the British Navy has decided their ships need to be
run along the lines of medium-sized companies. (feature)

2e Singular verb for plural

As terrorism and violence has ended, common problems such as
crime and skills shortages have loomed. (feature)

It is a tribute to the wit of the creators of 'Little Britain' that its
dystopian characters and Swiftian satire has struck a popular chord.
(leader)

They recall the Lawrence inquiry when the racism and incompetence
they took for granted was laid bare before an astonished public.
(feature)

The materials and technology used in aircraft design over the past 10
years has improved rapidly . . . (letter)

Lynne Truss, author of the bestselling *Eats, Shoots & Leaves*, told the
Times Educational Supplement . . . 'Correct punctuation and spelling
does have a bearing on people's success in life . . .' (news story)

2f Plural verb for singular

Jill Kelly, a former porn star who runs her own production company,
said: 'Anyone who continues to shoot at this point are complete
idiots.' (feature)

Bertrand Russell claimed that one of his literary models were the
Baedeker Guides, for their unambiguous clarity. (feature)

Suddenly I was under the most monstrous attack and everything I
valued – my home life, my future, my finances – were being
relentlessly threatened. (feature)

The yearly flurry of scandal, mischief-making, gossip and bitchiness
that surrounds the Booker or the Turner prize have become their
lifeblood. (feature)

Elsewhere everything from Janet Jackson's breast to bloggers on the
hunt for scalps in both press and broadcasting have shaken the
media's confidence. (feature)

3 Fewer and less

The more common mistake is 'less' for 'fewer':

> The issues go to the heart of the more-aid-and-less-questions formula for the continent's recovery. (feature)

> Less than 20% of people have access to toilet facilities. (fact box)

> This has been the subject of no less than three manifesto commitments. (feature)

> Tropicana offers no less than 13 different types of fresh orange juice to its American customers. (feature)

> Children who muck in with the cows and the pigs have less allergies than town kids. (feature)

But fewer should not be used for measurement of quantity:

> Mrs Miller won a payoff of £5m for fewer than three years of marriage. (news story)

> But with 68 millilitres fewer in the pack, consumer groups fear the price will remain the same – short-changing customers. (news story)

4 Tenses out of sequence

> Kevin Pietersen fell for a wonderful 71, as Australia restrict England at Edgbaston. (website picture caption)

It should be either 'fell' and 'restricted' or 'falls' and 'restrict'.

> Those who have toiled to earn their riches should be allowed to spend them as they chose. (column)

'Chose' should be 'choose'.

> He was in constant pain so he took too many pills and drunk far too much. (feature)

'Drunk' should be 'drank'.

He would happily downsize, quit London, find other work of some kind and leave me to do the childcare as long as he can still find time to paint. (column)

'Can' should be 'could'.

But it would have been a lot more fun if it was a bit more stupid. (book review)

'Was' should be 'had been'.

Subjunctive failure

The mayor, Alan Rose, suggested that Edinburgh-born Gill, who calls himself a London 'refugee', sticks to the cities. (feature)

The crucial thing is that the Lib Dems are not scared into ditching the essence of their politics. (feature)

I once met her in difficult circumstances, when she was successfully insisting that a piece about her contained no mention of her son by H.G. Wells . . . (literary column)

'Sticks' should be 'stick'; 'are' should be 'be'; 'contained' should be 'contain'. Alternatively use 'should' to make the meaning clear: 'should stick', 'should not be scared', 'should contain'.

5 May for might

If Jean-Paul Sartre were alive, which he isn't, and he gave advice, which he didn't, he may well have shed light on the correct use of the mobile phone. (feature)

Hoggard may never have become a cricketer if not for the late Phil Carrick. (fact box)

However, the centre elected to pass to Grewcock outside him when he may have scored himself. (rugby match report)

'The second incident may not have occurred if something had been done about the first.' (feature)

The Israeli security establishment came to believe that the Jewish state may not have survived without the relationship with the Afrikaners. (feature)

> The fact is, Oaten may well have got away with it. (feature)

The fact was, he didn't, so 'may' should have been 'might', as it should in all these examples.

6 One and you

> It was as if one's own internal contradictions were being conveniently staged for you. (feature)
>
> Just because the peak of a mountain is obscured by the weather, or the feebleness of one's own vision, it doesn't mean that you can't make a good guess that it is still bloody high up. (book review)
>
> [This book] makes one happily suspect that all you have to do to think like a philosopher is, well, think. (book review)
>
> One may have had no doubts that Berlin had a fine, discriminating mind; after reading even a few of his letters you realise that a good sign of a discriminating mind is that it knows how to be playful . . . (book review)
>
> When you edit a page, a section or even a whole newspaper you are essentially guessing – or using your judgment much as one might in a spot-the-ball competition. (feature)

Unless you want to sound formal, avoid 'one'; never mix 'one' and 'you'.

7 Saying it twice

> Those charged with designing new cruise ships and skyscrapers share a common bond. (column)

If a bond is shared it is held in common.

> Both Resolution and the Law Society have drawn up separate blueprints for reform. (news story)

'Separate' repeats 'both'.

> In the early nineteenth century they combined both of these. (feature)

'Both' is redundant again.

The press will have to self-censor itself. (feature)

'Self-' is redundant.

Sampson's purview is restricted solely to British institutions. (feature)

Cut 'solely'.

The main reason is due to the ever-growing problem of light pollution at night. (reader's letter)

Cut 'due to'.

Yet opinion polls show overwhelming support for the right to die in both Catholic and Protestant pews alike. (feature)

'Alike' repeats 'both'.

8 Whom for who

The party is being offered a peach in the petite form of Betsy, whom the Daily Mail decided was 'probably the most glamorous of the Tory leadership contenders' wives'. (feature)

Begin, whom MI6 believed was backed by the Soviet Union, planned to send five terrorist cells to Britain. (news story)

The sexual health charity Brook says taking away the right to confidential sexual health advice would be 'disastrous' for many teenagers, whom it argues will simply avoid asking for contraception or pregnancy advice . . . (news story)

Richard Cazaly (whom police now accept stabbed Abigail Witchalls) . . . (news story)

In all these cases 'whom' should be 'who'.

9 Pronoun abuse: I and me etc

Hope you can advise me on a problem which is causing a difference of opinion between my husband and I. (letter to gardening page)

'I' should be 'me'.

> As soon as we find him, he asks Adams and I to chat while he takes his pictures. (feature)

'I' should be 'me'.

> But I have seen him sitting at the dinner table, with we three, frozen-faced children, shouting at our mother . . . (feature)

'We' should be 'us'.

> Me and my house are not as glossy as once they were. (column)

'Me' should be 'I' (and come after my house, though that is etiquette not grammar).

> Us twirlies are people in possession of concessionary bus passes. (column)

'Us' should be 'we'.

> [Hilary] Armstrong complained that 'the trouble with people like you is you are so clever with words that us up north can't answer back'. (news feature)

'Us' should be 'we'.

10 And which etc

'That' followed by 'and which' is awkward, confusing and ungrammatical. Often it seems to be variation for its own sake:

> They introduced levels of comfort and sophistication to the west that had not been seen before, and which were not seen again for hundreds of years . . . (feature)

> A book that can be recommended by *Men's Health* – for whatever reason – and which can still insert such ideas into people's heads has to be welcomed. (book review)

In both cases the second clause is clearly similar to the first: there is no need to repeat 'that' but 'which' is both redundant and confusing in suggesting that the second clause has a different grammatical function from the first.

In other examples there may be a grammatical difference between the 'that' and the 'which' clause:

> Myth-making is a subject that fascinates Cornwell, and which he has explored before. (feature)
>
> Gold bought his first bass sax from Rollini, a battered instrument that had fallen out of a car, and which he had to spend a fortune on putting right. (feature)

But the more the second clause differs from the first, the stronger the argument for making it a separate point rather than tacking it on:

> Myth-making is a subject that fascinates Cornwell; he has often explored it before.
>
> Gold bought his first bass sax from Rollini, a battered instrument that had fallen out of a car, and (he) had to spend a fortune on putting it right.

The same treatment would improve this clumsy sentence:

> But it was *Hitler's War*, published in 1977, that was to gain him his greatest notoriety and in which he challenged the accepted historical version of the Holocaust. (feature)

Possibly worse than 'that and which' is 'which and who' – applied to the same noun:

> What this begins to suggest is that groups which are stigmatised, and who as a consequence do not have access to power, are most likely to become the victims of serial killers. (feature)

Another mistake is 'and who/which/where' without a 'who/which/where' in the first place:

> Martin Miller, founder of the famous Miller's antiques guides and who now makes gin . . . (feature)
>
> A country governed by a former Coke executive and where more Coca-Cola products are consumed per capita than anywhere else in the world. (news story)

These examples are not hard to rewrite:

> Martin Miller, who founded the famous Miller's antiques guides and (who) now makes gin . . .

> A country governed by a former Coke executive where more Coca-Cola products are consumed . . .

4
Grammar: problems and confusions

Grammar, syntax, usage, style – the terms are often confused. One person's grammatical howler is a simple matter of style for somebody else. This chapter covers common problems and confusions under the heading of 'grammar' – but not all the entries feature 'mistakes'.

A and an

Words with a silent 'h' such as 'honest' take 'an' instead of 'a':

an honest man

Unless your style book insists, don't use 'an' before such words as 'hotel', 'historian' and 'horrific', as in:

It was an horrific example of being in the wrong place at the wrong time. (feature)

Absolute adjectives

Don't misuse absolute adjectives such as:

absolute	ideal
basic	impossible
complete	obvious
empty	perfect
essential	pure
fatal	ultimate
final	unique
full	

A thing is either perfect or less than perfect. It cannot be 'more perfect' or 'most perfect'. It is similarly ludicrous to write 'more fatal' or 'more unique'.

After

'After' should mean what it says, that is 'later in time'; it should not be used as here:

> Bird flu has claimed its fifth human victim in three weeks after a 35-year-old woman died of the virus in southern Vietnam, officials said yesterday. (news story)

Flu claimed its fifth victim when, not after, the woman died.

And and but

See **Conjunctions to start sentences**, p. 37.

And which etc

See pp. 30–2.

Any

Like 'none' (see p. 43) 'any' can take either a singular or a plural verb. So there is nothing wrong with:

> Have any of the players turned up yet?

As

Be careful with 'as'. It has all sorts of uses including 'at the same time as'. It doesn't work here:

> Two arrested as pensioner is beaten to death in home.
> (news headline)

The arrests came a day after the attack, so 'as' should clearly be 'after'.

As and than

In comparisons 'as good' needs another 'as', just as 'better' needs 'than'. In this example the writer has used 'than' instead of 'as':

> Children whose parents smoke are one and a half times as likely to become asthmatic than those with non-smoking parents. (feature)

Often the second 'as' gets left out as in these three examples:

> The conditions under which young people from ethnic minorities are living in France are as bad, if not worse than those that black people suffered in Detroit in the 1960s and Brixton in the 1980s. (leader)

To correct this, put 'as' after 'bad' and a comma after 'than'. Or if the result sounds stilted, why not just say 'as bad as'?

> If the show goes ahead the list will be every bit – if not more – impressive than its British counterparts. (leader)

This is difficult to correct – better stop and start again.

> It is as bad or worse than 1976. (feature)

This one is easy: 'It is as bad as 1976, if not worse.'

Between

'Between' is most often used to show a relationship between two people or things. But it can be used for more than two as in:

> Lille is between Paris, Brussels and London.

It shouldn't be used instead of 'after' as here:

> During an interview for a magazine a decade and a half ago, I noted that Frayn, eating olives at the kitchen table, crossed to the sink to wash and dry his fingers between each light-green oval. (feature)

Replace 'between each light-green oval' by 'after each one'.

'Between' should be followed by 'and', not as in these three examples by 'or':

> Given the choice between Charles or an elected head of state, only 55% want him to be king. (feature)

> They will be making a choice between far more than just 'IDS', the ramrod-straight shadow defence secretary, or Ken, the beer-swilling and blokeish ex-chancellor and QC. (feature)

> . . . future women incumbents when they have to choose between this showy form of servitude or being depicted as unfashionably meek. (column)

'Between' should not be followed by a dash. Instead of 'between 1914–18', write either 'in 1914–18' or 'between 1914 and 1918'.

Bored (of)

Although 'bored of' is increasingly common it is better to stick with 'bored with'.

Both

See **Saying it twice**, pp. 28–9.

Centre around, in, on

See **Prepositions: the pitfalls**, pp. 45–6.

Compare like with like

Be careful to compare like with like. In the following example a problem is not a city:

> Thankfully, Scotland's gun problem has not yet reached the same scale as London, Manchester or Dublin.

Compare to and with

Use 'with' for routine comparisons – like with like, last year's figures with this year's. Use 'to' when the comparison itself makes a point as in:

Shall I compare thee to a summer's day?

Comprise (of)

'Comprise' does not take 'of'; the confusion is with 'consist of'. 'Is comprised of' is just as bad.

Conjunctions to start sentences

There is no problem with the use of 'and' and 'but' to start sentences. Whatever your English teacher may have said to the contrary, this isn't a grammatical mistake.

Nor is it bad grammar to write:

Because the food was awful they walked out.

But it is usually stronger to put the 'what' before the 'why':

They walked out because the food was awful.

See also **Fragments**, pp. 40–1.

Dangling modifier

See pp. 22–4.

Different from, than, to

'From' is the preferred preposition after 'different' but 'different to' is now commonly accepted in Britain; 'different than' has an American flavour.

Double negative

In modern standard English the double negative asserts the positive rather than emphasising the negative. Thus:

> I don't know nothing.

can mean that the speaker knows something rather than nothing:

> I don't 'know nothing'.

But in many people's speech it means the opposite. So beware of using the double negative in copy since it may be misunderstood.

Due to

'Due' is an adjective and is also used in adjectival phrases:

> The rent is *due*.
>
> The cancellation is *due to bad weather*.

Strict grammarians – and many house-style books – say that 'due to' may not be used to introduce an adverbial phrase; that what follows is a mistake:

> The train was cancelled *due to bad weather*.

So the best advice, whatever the railway companies may say, is: don't do it.

Equally

See **Saying it twice**, pp. 28–9.

Fed up (of)

Like 'bored', 'fed up' should be followed by 'with' not 'of'.

Few

Some nouns are only used as plurals or have a particular meaning in the plural. A story can have a 'moral', for example, but a person can't: they can only have 'morals' (ethical principles and conduct). So the following is wrong because 'few' suggests that 'morals' can be singular.

> Jack Shaftoe is magnificent, a swashbuckling hero with a foul mouth and few morals. (feature)

See also **'Fewer' and 'less'**, pp. 23, 26

Fewer and less

See p. 26.

Floating participle

See pp. 23–4.

Following

'Following' (originally a participle) is often used by journalists as a preposition to mean either 'after' or 'because of', as in:

> Following the rain the sun came out (after).
>
> The M4 is still closed following a pile-up (because of).

But it can be ambiguous as in:

> Following the success of New Labour in Britain, the French left hopes to do well in the elections.

Is there really a connection here or is the journalist trying to link two unrelated events in the reader's mind?

Be clear: instead of 'following' use either 'after' or 'because of'.

For you and I

See **Pronoun abuse**, pp. 29–30.

Fragments

Subordinate clauses starting with conjunctions such as 'although' and 'because' should not be used as stand-alone sentences as in:

> Isabel Spearman agrees that 'there is definitely a move away from diamonds on men's watches'. Although, she adds, they still sell well in Chester. (feature)

> Sex took over and obscenity became the new shocker. Although Muslims, it has to be said, don't go a bundle on either. (feature)

In both these examples the 'although' clause is logically part of the previous sentence.

Two things can make it harder to make sense of this kind of fragment. The first is a paragraph break before the conjunction:

> But the film also reminds us that his times are not our times.
>   Because Kinsey lived in an age that could be straightforwardly optimistic about the rewards offered by sexual frankness. (feature)

The second is extending the fragment by what could be seen as its main clause:

> We need to wake up to the fact that we're going to have to educate people – put it as part of the curriculum or provide parenting classes outside school. Because the children aren't happy, nobody's happy with this. (feature)

The reader expects the 'because' clause to be logically related to what follows: nobody is happy because the children aren't happy. But that isn't what the speaker means.

When there's both a paragraph break before the conjunction and extra material after the fragment, the reader is made to work even harder:

Lee wasn't a lager lout or a work-shy layabout. He was a conscientious, ambitious boy with a loving family; and his needless tragedy is a warning to us all.

Because drink has become our culture, it's an integral part of everyday life. (column)

From/to

'From' must be followed by 'to'. Do not write 'from 1939–45'. Write either 'in 1939–45' or 'from 1939 to 1945'.

Hopefully

Expressions such as 'hopefully' and 'generally speaking' are increasingly accepted in everyday journalism.

But avoid imprecision. In 'Generally speaking, grammar is important' and 'Hopefully, your punctuation will improve' the speaker/writer expresses an opinion, but it is not clear who shares it. Where it is important to be precise, always write:

I hope your punctuation will improve.

or:

Let *us* hope your punctuation will improve.

Lay and lie

Do not confuse 'lay' and 'lie'. 'Lay' is a transitive verb and so takes an object; 'lie' is an intransitive verb and does not:

Chickens *lay* eggs.

Waiters *lay* the table.

Soldiers *lay down* their arms.

but:

A sun-worshipper *lies down* on the beach.

Like and such as

Traditionally, 'like' makes a comparison whereas 'such as' introduces examples:

> Fruit trees, like flowers, need water.
>
> Fruit trees such as the plum and the cherry need pruning.

'Like' is now commonly used to introduce examples instead of 'such as':

> Fruit trees like the plum and the cherry need pruning.

But if there is any risk of confusion, stick to 'such as'. Also, remember that commas are essential with 'like' when a comparison is being made.

May for might

See pp. 27–8.

Meet

Do not use 'with' (still less 'up with') when 'meet' means 'come face to face with' (a person):

> Fred met Joan at the station.

Use 'with' when 'meet' means 'chance to experience' as in:

> He met with an accident.

Myself

The pronoun 'myself' has two uses.

> I sub myself.

is either reflexive, meaning:

> I sub my own copy.

or intensive – that is, it emphasises:

> I too am a subeditor.

Don't use 'myself' instead of 'me' in such sentences as:

> They asked Fred and me to work on the story.

None

'None' can take either a singular or a plural verb. In the examples that follow the plural would have been better:

> Our so-called representatives spat on the efforts that some of our foremost lawyers, scholars and parliamentarians had made to try to prevent the destruction of our most basic rights to justice. None of them is fit to run this country. (reader's letter)

> Almost none of them said she was happy and excited at being sexually mature. (feature)

> None of the characters is what they seem and fresh conspiracies are revealed at every turn. (book review)

> None of the killers has yet been brought to justice for their crimes. (book review)

No question/argument

Be careful with these phrases. A TV producer once wrote to the *Observer* to complain that he had been quoted as saying:

> The four are outspoken and there is no question we encouraged them to play up for the camera.

As he went on:

> What does this damaging ambiguity mean – that we did or that we didn't?

To convey the TV producer's meaning the quote should have read:

> There *was* no question *of our encouraging* them . . .

In the following examples 'there is no question/argument' looks as though it has the positive meaning 'it is certain':

> Bill T. Jones claims that he has mellowed with age, but there's no question that the trajectory of his 20-year career has been heavily fuelled by anger. (feature)

> There is no argument that Cliff's Eurovision classic, 'Congratulations', is the most irritating single of all time. (feature)

> There is no question that Dyke transformed the way the BBC felt about itself. (feature)

But confusion is possible with the similar-sounding but negative expression 'There is no question of/argument for [inviting him]'.

The following is worse than confusing – it is just nonsense (instead of 'argue' the verb should be 'dispute'):

> No one would argue that alcohol lowers inhibitions . . . (feature)

Number disagreement

See pp. 24–5.

One and you

See p. 28.

One word not two

Some hyphenated or separate pairs of words gradually become fused. Examples are 'forever', 'onto', 'subeditor', 'underway' and 'wicketkeeper'.

Only

Be careful with 'only': putting this word in the wrong place can affect the meaning of a sentence.

'I'm only here for the beer' is unlikely to be misunderstood, but what is meant by 'He only eats here on Tuesdays'? That on Tuesdays he refrains from drinking? Or that he eats here only on Tuesdays?

To be clear, put 'only' directly before the word or phrase it refers to.

Prepositions: the pitfalls

The most common mistake is to use the wrong preposition or to use one where it is not necessary. Here are some examples of commonly misused prepositions:

absent *from* (not *of*)
acquiesce *in* (not *to*)
affinity *between*, *with* (not *to*, *for*)
agree *on* (a point), *to* (a proposal), *with* (a person or opinion)
alien *from* (not *to*)
arise *from* (not *out of*)
bored: see p. 36
capacity *for* (not *of*)
centre *on/in* (not *around*)
compare: see p. 37
comprise: see p. 37
consider: no preposition (do not use *as*)
correspond *with* (a person), *to* (a thing)
credit *with* (not *for*)
die *of* (not *from*)
differ *from* (in comparisons, not *to* or *than*), *with* (a person when disagreeing)
different: see p. 37
dissent *from* (not *to*)
distaste *for* (not *of*)
fed up: see p. 38
glad *at* (a piece of news), *of* (a possession)
impatient *for* (a thing), *with* (a person)
independent *of* (not *from*)
indifferent *to*
martyr *for* (a cause), *to* (a disease)
meet: see p. 42
oblivious *of* (not *from* or *to*)
part *from* (a person), *with* (a thing)
prefer *to* (not *than* or *rather than*)
prevail *against* (a thing), *on* (a person)

> prevent *from*
> protest *at/against*
> reconcile *to* (a thing), *with* (a person)
> taste *of* (food), *for* (the arts and other things)

The American 'on' for 'the street', 'the team' etc is becoming increasingly common:

> The peculiar case of the law lords, the plutocrat, his 'Harvey Nichols wife' and the 'man on the street' (feature heading)

But stick to 'in' unless there is some point in the Americanism, eg to distinguish Smollensky's on the Strand (an American jazz joint) from the old fashioned English restaurant Simpson's in the Strand.

Most compound prepositions are an abomination. Avoid such expressions as:

> in connection with
> in regard to
> in relation to

Prepositions to end sentences

Ending a sentence with a preposition may sometimes be bad style but it is not bad grammar. As Winston Churchill once wrote (commenting on a clumsy sentence by a pedantic civil servant which avoided a prepositional ending): 'This is the sort of English up with which I will not put.'

So, where your ear tells you that a preposition can go at the end of the sentence, put it there.

Saying it twice

See pp. 28–9; see also **Redundant words**, p. 109.

Since

Be careful with 'since' which can mean both 'because' and 'from the time that'. The following sentence is at best confusing, at worst nonsensical:

They were the wrong gender since they were children.

It is intended to mean:

They have/had been the wrong gender since they were children.

Split infinitive

'To boldly go' is traditionally called a split infinitive: the infinitive ('to go') is split by an adverb ('boldly'). Modern grammarians have disputed this, arguing that the preposition 'to' does not form part of the infinitive, which therefore cannot be split. Others have pointed out that new verbs can be formed in English by putting an adverb before an existing verb ('to under-take', 'to over-throw') and that new expressions are formed in exactly the same way: 'to sexually harass', 'to verbally abuse'. Whatever else it is, a 'split infinitive' is not a grammatical mistake.

But a problem remains, partly because many writers and readers think there is one. Consider the following:

It is illegal deliberately to help someone to die. (column)

In several European countries it is a crime publicly to deny that the Holocaust ever took place. (feature)

He began actively to dislike me. (feature)

These are clear cases of split-infinitive avoidance: the writer doesn't want to put the adverb after 'to' and has made a simple sentence sound awkward.

Then there are cases of what seems like compulsive splitting:

'Older people tend to really cook their vegetables well, and if they overcook cauliflower they won't be getting those nutrients,' she said. (news story)

'Really' here belongs with 'well'.

To not have 'OJ' on the breakfast table is seen as something akin to a breach of human rights in the US. (feature)

> It is pettifogging to not use the word art to describe the cave paintings of Ice Age Europe. (feature)

What's wrong with the natural-sounding 'not to have/not to use'? After all, Hamlet didn't say 'To be or to not be'.

In deciding whether or not to put an adverb after 'to', ask yourself:

1   Is the adverb superfluous? Often it contributes nothing to the sense.
2   Would the adverb be better somewhere else in the sentence?
3   Would the sentence sound better/make better sense if it were rewritten?

If the answer to these questions is no, carry on 'splitting'.

Subjunctive failure

See p. 27.

Suffice (it) to say

'Suffice to say' should be 'suffice it to say' ('let it be enough to say'). So the following are wrong:

> Suffice to say that she is unlikely to apologise. (feature)

> (he's not 16st any more, suffice to say) (feature)

Superlatives

Don't use the superlative where you should use the comparative. For example, you can't have 'the least of two evils' or 'the best of two games' or 'the eldest of two brothers'. So the following are wrong:

> Who has the best command of the English language – Hay writers or *Guardian* journalists? (standfirst)

'Best' should be 'better'.

> Brown has the hardest job. He has to pretend that he agrees with Blair on virtually everything. (feature)

'Hardest' should be 'harder'.

Do not use a double superlative such as 'most fondest'.

If you qualify a superlative, as in 'the world's second longest river', be careful. The sentence 'The Amazon is the world's second longest river after the Nile' needs at least a comma after 'river' (brackets are better). Otherwise it means that the Amazon is the world's *third* longest river.

To put it another way, without a comma it would be more exact to write:

> The Amazon is the world's longest river after the Nile.

Tenses out of sequence

See pp. 26–7.

That and which

See p. 20.

They, their, them

There is no problem with using 'they', 'their' and 'them' to refer to a singular pronoun or noun as in:

> If anybody comes, tell them to wait.

Prefer this usage to 'he or she', 'he/she' etc.

Try to/and

After 'try' use the infinitive form not a conjunction. Try to write 'try *to* write' not 'try *and* write'.

Whether

'Whether' should not be followed by 'if' as in:

> This technical decision is the key signal of whether it's 'business as usual' or if Tony Blair is finally ready to start handing out the kind of medicine needed if Kyoto is to mean anything. (feature)

Which and that

See p. 20.

Whom for who

See p. 29.

With

Just as the preposition 'with' does not affect the verb in:

> Spelling, with grammar, is important.

so it does not affect the subject in:

> With her husband she faced the press.

Do not write:

> With her husband they faced the press.

5
Spelling

English spelling often defies logic. Why should we spell 'harass' with one 'r' and 'embarrass' with two? Why does 'mantelpiece' echo its Latin origin (*mantellum,* cloak) while 'mantle', the posh word for 'cloak', does not? Why does 'dependent' (the adjective) differ from 'dependant' (the noun)?

Whereas punctuation evolves, spelling does not. Whereas with grammar and punctuation you can sometimes argue a case for loose, colloquial usage, with spelling there is no way out. The word is either right or wrong – though some words are spelt in more than one way.

Nobody expects you to know how to spell all the words in the dictionary. The key thing is to avoid mistakes: learn to recognise the words you cannot spell and look them up. Use a spell-check system – but don't rely on it.

Words people get wrong

First, here's a list of words that many people can't spell. How about you?

abhorrence	authoritative	connoisseur
accidentally	auxiliary	consensus
accommodation		convertible
acquiescence	benefited	corpuscle
admissible	blamable	corroborate
annihilate	braggadocio	crucifixion
apartment	bureaucracy	
apostasy		debatable
asinine	Caribbean	definitely
asphyxiate	clamouring	descendant

desiccated
destructible
diagrammatic
diarrhoea
dignitary
discernible
dispel
dissatisfaction
dysentery

ecstasy
effervescence
eligibility
embarrass
emissary
exaggerate
exhilaration
expatriate

fallacious
forty
fulfilling
funereal

gaseous
guttural

haemorrhage
harass
heinous
herbaceous
hiccup
hierarchy
humorous
hygiene
hysterical

ideologist
idiosyncrasy
impresario
indispensable

indissoluble
innocuous
innuendo
inoculate
instalment
intestacy
iridescence

jeopardise

kitchenette

liaison
licentious
linchpin
liquefy
loquacious

maintenance
manoeuvre
mantelpiece
mayonnaise
meanness
Mediterranean
mellifluous
millennium
miniature
minuscule
miscellaneous
mischievous
moccasin

negotiate
nonchalant
noticeable

obeisance
occurred
omitted
oscillate

paraphernalia
pavilion
perspicacious
plummeted
predilection
privilege
profession
proprietary
pseudonym
publicly
pursue
Pyrenees

rarefy
recommend
reconnaissance
referred
restaurateur
resuscitate
riveted

sacrilegious
separate
statutory
straitjacket
supersede

targeted
tranquility

unforeseen
unnecessary
unparalleled

vacillate
verruca
veterinary
vociferous

withhold

Confusions

(See also Chapter 9, **Words**, p. 97.)

One reason why people misspell some words is that they confuse them with other words. There are three common kinds of confusion:

1   a word is confused with a shorter one that sounds the same

coconut	cocoa
consensus	census
dispel	spell
fulfil	full/fill
minuscule	mini
playwright	write
supersede	cede

2   a word is confused with a different one that sounds the same (homophone)

altar	alter
aural	oral
bail	bale
bait	bate
born	borne
breach	breech
cannon	canon
complement	compliment
cord	chord
counsel	council
curb	kerb
currant	current
deserts (runs away/ what is deserved)	desserts (puddings)
draft	draught
discreet	discrete
expatriate	ex-patriot
faze	phase
forbear	forebear
forego	forgo
foreword	forward
formally	formerly
geezer	geyser
grisly	grizzly

hanger	hangar
horde	hoard
lead (the metal)	led (the past participle)
lightening	lightning
metal	mettle
principal	principle
raise	raze
review	revue
sight	site
stationary	stationery
storey	story
swat	swot
toe	tow
way	weigh
yoke	yolk

3   a word used as one part of speech is confused with the same word used as another part of speech

Noun	Verb
practice	practise, *so also* practising, practised
licence	license, *so also* licensing, licensed
envelope	envelop, *so also* enveloping, enveloped.

Noun	Adjective
dependant	dependent

In one of the pairs listed above the words are pronounced differently:

Noun	Verb
en*ve*lope	en*ve*lop

If you find it difficult to distinguish between the common pairs *practic(s)e* and *licenc(s)e*, note that *advic(s)e* changes its pronunciation as well as spelling and remember the three pairs together:

Noun	Verb
advice	advise
practice	practise
licence	license

or remember the sentence:

Doctors need a licence to practise.

In this case the noun ('c') comes before the verb ('s').

Also note the opposite problem: two words with the same spelling that are pronounced differently and have different meanings:

*in*valid (as in chair)
invalid (as in argument)

de*serts* (runs away, what is deserved)
*de*serts (sand)

lead (the metal)
lead (the present tense)

re*ject* (verb)
*re*ject (noun)

pro*ject* (verb)
*pro*ject (noun)

I before e

Most people know the spelling rule 'i' before 'e' except after 'c'. This gives:

believe, niece, siege

and

ceiling, deceive, receive

But note exceptions such as:

caffeine, codeine, counterfeit, protein, seize

and, in the other direction:

species

Plurals

1   Nouns ending in a consonant followed by 'y' take 'ies' in the plural:

lady	ladies
penny	pennies
story	stories

But proper nouns take the standard 's' in the plural:

> the two Germanys
> three Hail Marys
> four Pennys in a class list

And nouns ending in a vowel followed by 'y' take the standard 's' in the plural:

donkey	donkeys
monkey	monkeys
storey	storeys

2   Most nouns ending in 'o' take the standard 's' but some common ones take 'es' in the plural:

> buffaloes, cargoes, dingoes, dominoes, echoes, embargoes, goes, heroes, mangoes, mottoes, negroes, noes, potatoes, tomatoes, tornadoes, torpedoes, vetoes, volcanoes

And some may be spelt either with 's' or 'es':

> archipelago, banjo, grotto, halo, innuendo, memento, mosquito, salvo

3   Nouns ending in 'f' usually take the standard 's' in the plural:

dwarf	dwarfs
handkerchief	handkerchiefs

(although 'dwarves' and 'handkerchieves' are found).

But note:

elf	elves

4   Some nouns that come from Greek, Latin or modern languages keep their original plural form:

addendum	addenda
alumna	alumnae
alumnus	alumni
bacillus	bacilli
chateau	chateaux
criterion	criteria
minimum	minima
phenomenon	phenomena
spectrum	spectra

In some cases both the original plural form and an anglicised version are used:

appendix	medium
appendices (used of books)	media (the press, etc)
appendixes (used of both	mediums (spiritualism)
books and the body)	
	memorandum
beau	memoranda
beaux	memorandums
beaus	
	plateau
bureau	plateaux
bureaux	plateaus
bureaus	
	stadium
cactus	stadia
cacti	stadiums
cactuses	
	syllabus
formula	syllabi
formulae (scientific)	syllabuses
formulas (general use)	
	terminus
fungus	termini
fungi	terminuses
funguses	
	virtuoso
index	virtuosi
indices (mathematics)	virtuosos
indexes (books)	

Be careful of confusing the singular with the plural when the latter form is more common as with:

graffito	graffiti
die	dice
stratum	strata

The plural of 'wagon-lit' is 'wagons-lits', not as some British dictionaries insist 'wagons-lit' or 'wagon-lits'; the plural of 'court martial' is 'courts martial'.

But note that plurals such as 'agenda', 'data' and 'media' are often treated as though they were singular. Check your house style.

Suffixes

1   One-syllable words with a short vowel and a single final consonant double it before a suffix that starts with a vowel.

fat	fatten, fatter
run	runner, running

2   So, too, do words with more than one syllable if the stress is on the final syllable.

begin	beginning, beginner
refer	referred, referral
prefer	preferred but note *preferable* (pronounced *preferable*)

3   But one-syllable words with a long vowel or double vowel do not double the final consonant.

seat	seated, seating
look	looking, looked

4   Nor do words with more than one syllable if the stress is before the final syllable.

proffer	proffering, proffered
benefit	benefiting, benefited
leaflet	leafleting, leafleter

5   Exceptions to these rules include most words ending in '1':

cavil	cavilling
devil	devilled (but *devilish*)
level	levelled
revel	reveller
travel	traveller

but:

parallel	paralleled

and some words ending in 'p' or 's':

worship	worshipped
bus	buses
gas	gases

while some words ending in 's' are optional:

bias	biased or biassed
focus	focused or focussed

House style determines whether the extra 's' is added.

6   Sometimes the stress changes when a noun is used as a verb:

format   formative but formatted (in computer speak)

Dictionaries generally give:

combat   combatant   combative   combated

But there is an argument for 'combatted' on the grounds that some people pronounce it that way. (You can, of course, avoid the problem altogether by using 'fight' as a verb instead of 'combat': it's one character shorter.)

7   Whether 'learn' becomes 'learnt' or 'learned', 'dream' becomes 'dreamt' or 'dreamed', is a matter of house style. But 'earn' can only become 'earned'.

8   Words ending in a silent 'e' keep it if the suffix begins with a consonant:

safe	safety
same	sameness

But note that there are common exceptions:

due	duty
true	truly
awe	awful (but awesome)
wide	width

And some words are optional:

acknowledg(e)ment, judg(e)ment

9   Words ending in a silent 'e' drop it if the suffix begins with a vowel:

bake	baking
sane	sanity

but:

change	changeable
mile	mileage

Note that 'y' here acts as a vowel:

gore   gory
ice   icy

10   Sometimes keeping or losing the silent 'e' makes it possible to distinguish two words with different meanings:

dying   (the death)
dyeing   (clothes)

linage   (payment by the line)
lineage   (descent)

singing   (musically)
singeing   (burning)

swinging   (from a tree)
swingeing   (heavy)

Agreement

A few words taken from French have an extra 'e' for the feminine form:

blond(e), brunet(te), confidant(e), débutant(e).

Note that in French an adjective agrees with its noun not the person the adjective refers to. Thus (since hair has no gender in English):

A blonde woman has blond hair.

This logical point is made in several house-style books – but generally ignored.

'Chaperon(e)' is a curiosity. In French *chaperon* exists only as a masculine noun; in English the (false) feminine form 'chaperone' is far more common.

Spelling mistakes

There are two kinds of published spelling mistakes nowadays: ones caused by over-reliance on spell-checkers (homophones) and ones caused by the failure to use spell-checkers (straightforward errors). The first can be amusing; the second are a sign of carelessness and contempt for the reader.

For some reason, the book-buying public seems to regard the *concensus* of a panel as more objectively reliable than a single identified critic. (feature)

Such a mutiny would have been *lead* from the top.
(blog published in newspaper)

The dominant but *floored* ideologies of Marxist and Whig histories . . .
(feature)

'I feel all right, but I'm still smoking like a *trouper*' (feature)

Some might say this passenger got more than his just *desserts*.
(feature)

The House of Commons lives by the *principal* that all of its members are constrained by the same standing orders. (column)

He adopts a *course* Aussie accent. (feature)

One of the most important dates in the hunting *calender*. (feature)

He *parleyed* that into a governorship in the service of the Sikh king of the Punjab. (book review)

It isn't a cardinal or mortal sin, but a *venal* one. (column)

Russell Thomson, the British *counsel* in Alicante . . . (feature)

I had been collecting these letters for more than a decade, *prying* them from Bellow's wives, friends, lovers . . . (literary column)

During the 1990s there was quite *literary* no immigration policy in the country. (feature)

He forsakes the comforts of Strangers' Bar to *bathe* their baby, Donald. (feature)

Australia had the *moral* and the shape to hit back with a series of late attacks. (sports report)

My brother is a living textbook definition of Yorkshire *stoney*-facedness.
(column)

Not everyone writes with such *forebearance*. (book review)

The Nazis regarded Von Stauffenberg's mentor George as one of the artistic and spiritual *forbears* of their movement. (feature)

If some, more upmarket, forms of prostitution are *permissable*, can we really expect to crack down effectively on the rest? (feature)

Mr Justice Clarke also ruled the evidence was *inadmissable*. (news report)

Mr Haylett whose complaint to *Tribune* elicited first a *humourous* correction. (diary item)

When I'm invited to dress *glamourously* I am naturally flattered. (column)

Johnny Grant, 82, serves as Hollywood's *honourary* mayor. (news report)

So where I was *cossetted* by four chefs and one superb restaurant boss, I was reduced to two chefs. (restaurant review)

Rivetting account of how Chess turned this new sound into a multi-million-dollar industry that changed the world. (book review)

Miller's reporting style was *appaling*. (column)

Lynch perhaps imagines that the same broad associative *license* extends to prose. (book review)

Some *idiosyncracy* of their digital instructions. (feature)

UK passenger *journies* to increase from 200 million to 500 million a year by 2030. (feature)

What would his ancestor make of the politicking and half-truths that are bread and butter to his *discendent*? (book review)

6
Punctuation

The point of punctuation is to make writing easier to read. It is the counterpart of the pauses and inflections that help to make speech understandable. But it doesn't necessarily follow that everywhere you would pause in speech you should punctuate in writing. And sometimes the strength of a punctuation mark differs from the length of the equivalent pause in speech.

Ideally, punctuation should be based on sound logical principles. But don't try to force your punctuation practice into a format that defies current usage.

Punctuation practice is constantly changing. For example, sentences are shorter than they used to be so there are now more full stops in text. But in general there is less punctuation.

- Since sentences are shorter there are fewer intermediate stops such as commas.

- Full stops are no longer seen as necessary to mark abbreviations and contractions.

- In headlines, standfirsts and captions, the final full stop is rare.

- Many publications no longer use capital letters for expressions such as the continent (of Europe) and the chancellor of the exchequer.

- Apostrophes are less common to mark plurals, as in 'dos and don'ts', which once had three apostrophes and now has only one.

- Some previously hyphenated words such as 'wicket-keeper' and 'e-mail' are often printed as single words.

The four main stops

These are: the comma, the semicolon, the colon and the full stop. Of these the comma is the weakest and the full stop the strongest. The colon used to be seen as a stronger stop than the semicolon. Now the semicolon lies midway between a comma and a full stop while the colon has a series of specialist uses.

Comma

1   Use the comma to separate a series of words of the same kind:

> The reporter should always write clear, concise, accurate English.

But do not use the comma when a series of adjectives is cumulative:

> He ordered a rich chocolate sponge cake.

2   Use the comma to separate a series of phrases of the same kind:

> His writing was more refined, more intellectual, more Latinate, than Smith's.

3   Use a comma before the 'and' at the end of a list where it is necessary for readability:

> The menu was soup, fish and chips, and trifle.

But not where it doesn't:

> The menu was soup, fish, and trifle.

At the end of simple lists this 'serial' comma between 'fish' and 'and' (also called the Oxford comma, because the Oxford University Press favours it) is pointless and unnecessary.

4   Use the comma to mark off words that address somebody or something:

> Come on, City.

5   Use the comma, where appropriate, to mark off words or phrases such as 'however', 'for example', 'in fact', 'of course':

> However, with punctuation it pays to be careful.

6   Use the comma to mark off a word in parenthesis:

> Born in Brixton, south London, he became prime minister.

7   Use the comma to mark off a phrase in parenthesis:

> Norman Mailer's first novel, *The Naked and the Dead*, was a bestseller.

Do not use the comma where the phrase is essential to the meaning of the sentence:

> Norman Mailer's novel *The Naked and the Dead* was a bestseller.

Here commas would mean that Mailer had written only one novel.

Also note the difference between '*the prime minister, Tony Blair,*' and '*Tony Blair, the prime minister,*' (both parenthetical, so commas) and '*prime minister Tony Blair*' and '*the Labour politician Tony Blair*' (not parenthetical, so no commas).

8   Use the comma to mark off a clause in parenthesis:

> The paper's subs, who were in their shirt sleeves, worked fast.

Do not use the comma where the clause is essential to the meaning of the sentence:

> The subs who were in their shirt sleeves worked fast; those who were wearing summer blouses worked even faster.

(See **Clauses**, p. 20.)

But note the example below, which is an exception to this rule:

> He who can, does. He who cannot, teaches.

9   Use the comma, where necessary, to mark off an introductory phrase or clause:

> Because of the appalling weather, conditions for holidaymakers were described as 'intolerable'.

Where a phrase or clause that needs commas follows a conjunction such as 'but' or 'and', the first comma is now considered to be optional:

> Fred tried to get up but (,) because he was tired and emotional, he failed.

10   Use the comma, where two sentences are joined by a conjunction, if you want to lengthen the pause:

> He wanted to leave the party, but his friend detained him.

Do not use the comma where the subject of the two sentences is the same:

> He wanted to leave but didn't.

Do not use the comma between sentences where there is no conjunction: Avoid:

> He wanted to leave, his friend detained him.

But note the example below of a series of short sentences where the comma can be used:

> I came, I saw, I conquered.

11   For the use of commas in quotes see Chapter 7, **Reporting speech**, p. 83.

Semicolon

1   Use the semicolon between sentences, with or without a conjunction, as a longer pause than a comma and a shorter one than a full stop:

> The rumour was that the king was dead; the people believed it.
>
> There will be an inquest, of course; but the matter will not end there.

2   Use the semicolon to separate longer items in a list, particularly if the items themselves need further punctuation by commas:

> Punctuation marks include the full stop, which is the strongest stop; the semicolon, which is weaker; and the comma, which is weakest of all.

Colon

1   Use the colon, in preference to the comma, to introduce full-sentence quotes:

> He said: 'Punctuation is difficult.'

2   Use the colon to introduce lists:

>   All of them were dead: Bill, Jack, Ted and Willie.

3   Use the colon between two sentences where the second explains or justifies the first:

>   Keep your language uncluttered: it reads more easily.

4   Use the colon between two sentences to mark an antithesis:

>   Man proposes: God disposes.

5   Use the colon in a picture caption to connect the person or object in the picture with the rest of the caption:

>   Victorious: Napoleon

>   Napoleon: 'Victory is ours'

Full stop (full point, period)

Use the full stop in text to mark the end of a sentence. You do not need to use full stops after headlines, standfirsts, captions and other forms of displayed type: remember that white space punctuates.

The paragraph break

The paragraph break can be called the fifth main stop since it is one stage stronger than the full stop. As with other forms of punctuation its main purpose is to make reading easier. A new paragraph can signal a change of subject or give the reader a rest.

Journalism is inclined to use short pars partly because it is typeset in columns of a few words to the line (rather than across the page as in this book), so that a given number of words looks longer on the page. And journalists write knowing that they need to struggle to catch and keep the reader's attention.

The shorter the par the more it stands out.

Popular papers and magazines use shorter pars than upmarket publications because they fight harder for the reader's attention; and tabloids have shorter pars because they have narrower columns. News stories are written in shorter pars than features because they are less of a read, more of a series of facts. They assume a reader in a hurry with a short attention span.

Commentators from outside journalism sometimes criticise its short pars for producing a jerky, disjointed effect. But they miss the point that in news writing this is part of the style.

A news intro in both tabloids and broadsheets is usually a stand-alone sentence written to give the gist of the story.

After the intro the story starts all over again and is told in greater detail, with each stage having a new par. When you have written your intro, the best guide to structuring a news story is to answer your reader's questions in the order you think they would ask them.

In many news stories disparate elements are brought together; each one needs its own par.

The reporter and the news sub are not expected to manipulate the material so that the copy gains an artificial smoothness. In news – as in life – there are often abrupt entrances and loose ends left lying around.

A feature, by contrast, should flow. Each par should be written to follow the one before so that the reader is seduced into continuing to read whatever their interest in the content. Thus a feature often has bridges linking one par with another and its pars are usually longer than those in news.

But the occasional short one can have a dramatic effect.

It is hard to give general advice about how long (or short) your pars should be. But:

- If your news intro goes beyond 25 words you should think again and try to rewrite it.

- In news a par that goes beyond three sentences/10 lines is likely to be too long.

- Never quote two people in the same par: always start a new one for the second quote.

- Never tack a new subject onto the end of a par.

- In features avoid a succession of short pars – unless you want to produce a jerky effect.

Quotation marks (quote marks, quotes)

1   Use quote marks for direct speech: see Chapter 7, **Reporting speech**, p. 83.

2   Use quote marks for extracts from written reports, following the same rules as for speech.

3   Use quote marks in a headline to show that an assertion is made by somebody in the story rather than by your publication: this can be vital in court stories.

4   Whether you use double or single quotes in text is a matter of house style, but in headlines always use single quotes.

5   For quotes within quotes use double inside single, and vice versa:

   He said: 'I really meant to say, "I'm sorry."'

   He said: "I really meant to say, 'I'm sorry.'"

   Note that a comma rather than a colon introduces the second quote.

6   Quote marks are sometimes used for the titles of books, plays etc – check your house style.

7   Quote marks are sometimes used to emphasise or draw attention to particular words or phrases, to identify slang or technical expressions.

   Do not do this unless it is essential for clarity.

   Avoid:

   That double-glazing salesman is a 'cowboy'.

   Either use slang because it fits the context or find another expression.

8   Whether you use single or double quote marks, be consistent. Do not use one form for quoting people and another for book titles and other uses.

Parentheses

1   For a routine, weak parenthesis use commas (see p. 65).

2   To mark a strong but unemphatic parenthesis, usually to explain rather than comment, use round brackets (confusingly they are often called 'parentheses'):

> National Union of Journalists (NUJ)
>
> five miles (about eight kilometres)
>
> Don't call a noisy meeting a shambles (the word means 'slaughterhouse').

When a parenthesis forms part of a sentence, the full stop comes after the second bracket (as here). (But when the whole sentence is a parenthesis, as here, the full stop comes before the second bracket.)

3   To mark a parenthesis added by the writer or editor to explain or comment, use square brackets:

> The novelist writes: 'He [the main character] dies in the end.'
>
> 'The standard of your spelling and grammer [sic] is terrible.'

4   To mark a strong, emphatic parenthesis, usually to comment rather than explain, use dashes:

> John Smith – the man's a fool – is staying here.

5   The mark that guides the reader to a footnote can be used in journalism.*

Other marks

Dash

1   Use dashes to mark a strong parenthesis (see above).

_____

* But don't overdo it.

2   Use the dash, where appropriate, to introduce an explanation or to sum up:

> Journalism has many forms – newspaper, periodical, broadcast.

Note that the colon here would do as well – the dash is less formal.

> Newspaper, periodical, TV and radio – these are the main forms of journalism.

3   Use the dash to add emphasis or mark a surprise:

> This is the point – there's no escaping it.

> You'll never guess who wrote the story – Fred Bloggs.

4   Use the dash to mark a change of direction or interruption, particularly in speech:

> 'I suppose – but what's the use of supposing?'

> 'I suppose –' 'Why are you always supposing?'

5   Use either the em (long) dash or the en (short) dash, according to house style.

6   Do not confuse the dash with the hyphen (see below).

Hyphen

1   Use the hyphen for figures written out:

> ninety-nine

2   Use the hyphen, where appropriate, for compound words such as:

(a)   titles:

> vice-president

(b)   prefix plus adjective:

> extra-marital sex

The sex takes place outside marriage. By contrast 'extra marital sex' suggests married couples working overtime.

(c)   adjective plus adjective:

  red-hot coals

The first adjective modifies the second.

(d)   adverb plus adjective used before the noun:

  a well-known fact

but:

  The fact is well known.

There is no need for a hyphen after adverbs ending in '-ly' because their meaning is clear. Distinguish between:

  a close-knit band of men

and:

  a closely knit band of men

(e)   adjective plus noun:

  a black-cab driver

This refers to the driver of a black (licensed) taxi. By contrast 'black cab driver' may suggest that the driver is black.

(f)   noun plus noun:

  a black cab-driver

This makes it clear that the driver, rather than the cab, is black.

(g)   noun plus preposition plus noun:

  mother-in-law

(h)   verb plus preposition used as noun:

  get-together

When used as a verb, the word does not take the hyphen:

  We get together at a get-together.

(i)   prefix plus proper noun or adjective:

  pre-Christian

(j)   prefix plus word to distinguish between meanings:

re-creation (*making something again*) recreation (*leisure*)

(k)   two words that together make a clumsy or ugly juxtaposition:

supra-intestinal

Caithness-shire

3   Use the hyphen to mark word breaks at the ends of lines. Note:

(a)   with unjustified setting (no right-hand margins) hyphens are less common

(b)   avoid a succession of word breaks

(c)   when you hyphenate, try to break words into their constituent parts

(d)   avoid making unintentional words such as *anal-ysis*.

Problem

Double compounds: should it be 'a New York-based writer', a 'New-York-based writer' or 'a New York based writer'?

Solution: Use the first formula unless there is a risk of misunderstanding; then turn the expression round to avoid using the hyphen.

Apostrophe

1   Use the apostrophe to show that something is left out of a word:

don't

fo'c's'le

Do not use the apostrophe to show that a word has been shortened.

Avoid:

thro', 'phone, the '60s

Either use the word in full ('through') or in its shortened form without the apostrophe ('phone').

2   Use the apostrophe to mark the possessive:

> women's liberation, lamb's liver, for goodness' sake

Putting the apostrophe in the right place distinguishes singular from plural:

> a dolls' house

assumes more than one doll

> the doll's hairdo

does not.

3   The possessive use is extended to cover 'for' as well as 'of', as in 'children's books' (those written for children).

4   Use the apostrophe *where necessary* to make a plural clear:

> Mind your p's and q's.

But not where typography does the job:

> Mind your Ps and Qs/Mind your *ps* and *qs*.

Do not use the apostrophe for routine abbreviations in the plural. Particularly avoid the greengrocer's apostrophe:

> Tom's 40p

Instead of the price of tomatoes, it looks like Tom's pocket money.

Apostrophe problems

1   Place names: 'King's Langley' *but* 'Kings Norton'.

Solution: follow usage and use reference books.

2   Names of organisations: 'Harrods' but 'Christie's'.

Solution: follow the organisation's own style (check the phone directory) unless it is illiterate: do not write 'womens'.

3   The extra 's': 'Thomas'' or 'Thomas's'?

Solution: follow sound – if the extra 's' is sounded, include it:

> St Thomas's hospital, Marx's writings

If there is no extra 's' in speech, do not add it.

Dégas' art, Socrates' philosophy

are correct.

4   The double apostrophe:

Fred's book's title

Solution: avoid it where possible; prefer:

the title of Fred's book

5   The apostrophe with a title in quotes:

the point of 'Ode to Autumn's' imagery

Solution: avoid – either don't use quotes for titles or write:

the point of the imagery of 'Ode to Autumn'

Question mark (query)

Use the query after a direct question:

Are you coming?

He asked: 'Are you coming?'

The query is inside the quote marks because the whole question is quoted:

Have you read 'Ode to Autumn'?

The query is outside the quote marks because the question is not part of the quote.

Why is everybody always picking on me?

Although the question may be rhetorical – no answer is expected – it still needs a query.

Common query mistakes

1   Including a query in indirect speech:

> He asked if I was coming?

2   Misplacing the query in direct quotes:

> He asked: 'Are you coming'?

Exclamation mark (screamer)

Use the screamer only when it is essential to mark an exclamation:

> Ooh, I say!

Do not use the screamer to make comments, signal jokes or mark rhetorical questions.

Dots (ellipsis, leader dots . . .)

1   Use three dots to show that something has been omitted, for example from a written quotation. But when you edit quotes in writing up an interview, there is no need to use the dots each time you omit a word.

2   Use three dots to mark a pause:

> I suppose . . . but what's the use of supposing?

3   Use three dots to lead the reader from one headline to another when they are linked:

> Not only . . .

> . . . but also

4   Use dots in charts and tables to make them more readable.

Slash (oblique /)

Use the slash in website addresses and to mean either, as in 'and/or'.

Asterisk (*)

Use the asterisk (rarely) for footnotes and, in papers where this is style, to avoid printing a swear word in full – f*** (see **Four-letter words**, p. 104.).

Blob (bullet point •)

Use the blob either to emphasise items in a list or to mark that a separate story has been added to the main piece.

Punctuation mistakes

How much damage is done to readability by bad punctuation? Try this from a cricket report:

> Kettles boiled Fred.

Baffling or what? The previous sentence reads:

> There was time for Flintoff to romp to 33 from 29 balls, belting his last ball into the Tavern Stand before charging in for his tea as if called by his mum.

And the sentence should read:

> 'Kettle's boiled, Fred.'

Apostrophe

A common apostrophe mistake is to add an 's' before, instead of after, the apostrophe:

> This might make things a bit clearer in peoples' minds. (feature)

> Adultery would attract 10 points, rising to 18 if with the childrens' nanny. (humorous column)

> Sitting on the womens' committee . . . the Conservative Womens' National Council. (feature)
>
> The vast profits from selling bottled water are unlikely to be felt much at the waters' source. (feature)

Another one is to put the apostrophe before the final 's' of a word, rather than after it:

> Julia Robert's current Broadway performance . . . (feature)
>
> Any of Engel's homes . . . (feature)
>
> Sea bass at £14.95 and calve's liver and bacon at £12.95 . . . (feature)

Sometimes the apostrophe shouldn't be there at all:

> But who's duty is it to get rid of the rubbish? (column)

Comma

In the following examples the commas are wrong:

> The Nazi propagandist and anti-semite, David Irving . . . (column)

This suggests there is only one Nazi propagandist and anti-semite.

> He co-founded with José Ángel Ezcurra the paper, *Triunfo* (Triumph). (obit)

This suggests there is only one paper.

> The feminist writer, Beatrix Campbell, has indicted a region. (feature)

This suggests there is only one feminist writer.

> President John Kennedy had appointed the labour educator, Esther Peterson, to head the Women's Bureau. (obit)

This suggests there is only one labour educator.

> Most major towns and cities have a resident drug emporium selling a selection of legal, mind-altering drugs. (news story)

Here the comma is wrong because the adjectives are cumulative: the mind-altering drugs are legal.

> Gail and Frank were like the only two sane people in that hideous town. (feature)

Like, used in this way, needs to be marked off by commas – or the meaning of the sentence is that Gail and Frank resemble the two sane people.

> This week he delivered another shock to his Republican base by appointing a Democrat and a Kennedy to boot as his chief of staff. (news story)

Commas – or dashes – are needed after 'Democrat' and 'boot'.

> We tend to hide, not joke, about the number of units of alcohol we consume. (feature)

The second comma is in the wrong place: it should be after 'about' not 'joke'.

> Trollope grew up in Reigate, Surrey, and books were a very basic, yet vivid part of her early life. (feature)

The comma after 'basic' requires another after 'vivid'.

> Poppy and its more lucrative derivatives opium and heroin, grease every wheel of the local economy. (feature)

The comma after 'heroin' requires another after 'derivatives'.

> When at the end of the first preview, the audience rose to their feet to acclaim Kate's performance, I was distracted by the producer. (feature)

The comma after 'preview' requires another after 'when'.

> Beauties have a nicer time, better jobs, even babies prefer them. (feature)

The comma after 'jobs' should be a dash.

There were grassroots women's liberation groups inspired by civil rights, there was student activism, opposition to the Vietnam war, the mobilisation of women on welfare and rebellions in the black ghettos. (obit)

The comma after 'rights' should be a semicolon.

Dash

She is 'certainly not political', according to her mother – and her husband's constituents – are quite happy that she isn't so. (feature)

The second dash suggests a false parenthesis: delete.

The Pope's time at the seminary between 1939–1941 has been shrouded in controversy because of his membership of the Hitler Youth. (news story)

'Between' should be followed by 'and', not a dash; and in the next example 'from' should be followed by 'to', not a dash:

I lived in Peshawar covering the war in Afghanistan from 1988–89 . . . (feature)

Hyphen

The most common mistake is to insert a hyphen after an -ly adverb when it can have no function:

The study confirms that newly-wedded bliss is the happiest time. (news story)

They should have been presented in a heavily-chased casket. (column)

The Conservative opponent was left flapping around like a freshly-landed plaice. (news story)

'This is probably the most eagerly-anticipated World Cup of all time.' (feature)

The Collins Dictionary (2003) makes this mistake in its entry for 'pharming':

> the practice of rearing or growing genetically-modified animals or plants in order to develop pharmaceutical products

In the following cases the hyphen also has no function and should be removed:

> The extraordinary growth of the women's-liberation movement . . . (obit)

> He has only recently returned to the first-team. (news story)

> He had the humanity to look sternly into the middle-distance when lives were lost. (feature)

By contrast, in the following cases, a hyphen is necessary:

> In the last five years there has been an increased acceptance of the need to formally risk assess school trips. (feature)

'Risk-assess' would make the sense clearer.

> Big Brother has suggested they try some animal role play exercises. (feature)

'Role-play' would be better.

> Milk producing gland of cows etc (crossword clue)

A hyphen is needed after 'milk'.

> How police gay rights zealotry is threatening our freedom of speech (comment headline)

A hyphen is needed between 'gay' and 'rights'.

Headlines often present a particular problem because of their layout. In the following cases there should logically be hyphens after 'bus', 'accident' and 'gay' – but there can't be for visual reasons. *Solution*: rewrite the headline.

Driving lessons for bus
loving leader

Crackdown
on accident
claims
'cowboys'

US bishop
takes on gay
sex critics

7
Reporting speech

Reporting speech accurately and clearly is an essential journalistic skill. You must be able to handle both direct quotes and indirectly reported speech.

Direct quotes

1   When you quote a person for the first time, introduce them before the quote:

> John Smith, the leader of the council, said: 'Of course, I refuse to resign.'

Because the quote is a complete sentence, it is introduced by a colon and starts with a capital letter; the full stop comes before the second quote mark.

2   Subject to house style you can use 'says' instead of 'said':

> John Smith, the leader of the council, says: 'I refuse to resign.'

3   Subject to house style you can use the short form 'council leader':

> Council leader John Smith says: 'I refuse to resign.'

But note:

(a)   the style works best when the description is short, say, up to three words: 'company managing director John Smith' is acceptable; 'chairman and managing director John Smith' is probably too long

(b)   since the style is supposed to be short and snappy, avoid prepositions such as 'of': 'leader of the council John Smith' is nonsense

(c)   since the short description functions as a title, it does not combine well with a real title: 'council leader Dr John Smith' looks and sounds awful and should be avoided.

4   Later in the story variation is possible. Either:

> He said: 'I have done nothing wrong.'

or:

> 'I have done nothing wrong,' he said.

Because the quote is a complete sentence, the comma comes before the second quote mark, replacing the full stop in the original.

5   Where the quote is longer than a sentence, put 'he said' either before the quote or after the first complete sentence, not at the end of the quote:

> 'I'm baffled by the accusations,' he said. 'In fact, I can't see what all the fuss is about.'

6   In features, but not in news, you may break the sentence for effect:

> 'I'm baffled,' he said, shaking his head, 'by the accusations.'

7   Where a quote continues for more than a paragraph, repeat the quote marks before each new quoted paragraph:

> 'I'm baffled by the accusations,' he said. 'In fact, I can't see what all the fuss is about.
>
> 'I really don't know what to do about the terrible mess I seem to be in.'

There is no closing quote mark after the word 'about'.

8   In general avoid inverting 'Smith' and 'said'. Never write:

> Said Smith: 'I will never resign.'

An acceptable use of inversion is where 'Smith' follows the quote and in turn is followed by an explanatory phrase or clause:

'I will never resign,' said Smith, who has been leader of the council for 10 years.

9   You may want to quote a particular word or phrase:

He described himself as 'really baffled'.

Note that here, because the quote is not a complete sentence, the full stop comes after the quote mark.

A word of warning: don't litter your copy with bitty quotes; in general try to quote complete sentences.

10   For quotes within quotes use double quote marks inside single and vice versa:

He said: 'I really meant to say, "I'm sorry." '

He said: "I really meant to say, 'I'm sorry.' "

Note that in both cases a comma rather than a colon introduces the second, enclosed quote.

11   Use a new paragraph when you quote a person for the first time.

Reported speech

1   The traditional way of reporting speech indirectly is to move most tenses one stage back. Thus the direct quote 'I support electoral reform' becomes:

He said he supported electoral reform.

'I have always supported electoral reform' becomes:

He said he had always supported electoral reform.

'I will always support electoral reform' becomes:

He said he would always support electoral reform.

With the simple past there is usually no change. 'I supported electoral reform until I became leader of the party' becomes:

He said he supported electoral reform until he became leader of the party.

(But it is possible to put 'had' before 'supported' for clarity/ emphasis.)

This traditional style has the clear advantage that succeeding paragraphs in the appropriate tense are clearly identified as reported speech:

> He said he started supporting electoral reform as a student and did so until he became leader of the party.

> Whatever anybody else said, he was still committed to change.

Always follow the correct sequence of tenses: 'is/has' becomes 'was/had'.

2   Journalists increasingly use 'he says' instead of 'he said' for reported speech, even in news stories. Thus 'I support electoral reform' becomes:

> He says he supports electoral reform.

'I supported electoral reform until I became leader of the party' becomes:

> He says he supported electoral reform until he became leader of the party.

Subject to house style you can use this form – but remember that 'he said' must be used in reporting set-piece events such as speeches, public meetings, courts and tribunals.

3   An advantage of 'he says' over 'he said' is that there is no difficulty in distinguishing between the present 'I support electoral reform' and the past 'I supported electoral reform': the tense remains the same in reported speech. But if you have to use 'he said', it is better to be clear and clumsy than ambiguous. So, where there is the risk of misunderstanding, write:

> He said he supports electoral reform.

4   Unless there is a good reason, do not mix your tenses. Do not write 'he said' in one sentence and 'he thinks' in the next.

5   Do not write: 'Speaking at the meeting the speaker said . . .' Instead write:

> The speaker told the meeting . . .

6   Do not follow the fashion of always leaving 'that' out. Leave it out
     where the subject remains the same:

> He says he supports electoral reform.

Where the subject changes 'that' is optional:

> He says (that) his opponent supports electoral reform.

But leave 'that' in after words such as 'claims' and 'admits' that have
another meaning. Avoid:

> He claims the prize of electoral reform is worth fighting for.

7   Also, be careful with punctuation. As it stands, the sentence 'John
     Smith admitted Fred Brown wanted to hit him and did so' could
     mean several different things:

(a)   John Smith admitted that Fred Brown wanted to hit him and
      that he did so.

(b)   John Smith, admitted Fred Brown, wanted to hit him and
      did so.

(c)   John Smith admitted [let in] Fred Brown, wanted to hit him
      – and did so.

General points

1   In general, where speakers say things that are nonsensical, obscure
     or ambiguous, report their words indirectly, telling the reader what
     they intended to say. For example, do not use 'refute' to mean 'deny'
     since many people think that to refute an argument is to show that
     it is false. So if a director says 'I refute your claim that my company
     is corrupt', write:

> The director denied that his company was corrupt.

2   Do not be afraid of repeating 'he says' or 'he said' in your story. The
     reader is far more likely to be irritated by awkward variants such as
     'commented', 'remarked' and 'stated'. Above all, be careful with
     'claimed', 'asserted' (negative) and 'pointed out', 'explained' (posi-
     tive). Use them only where they are accurate and add weight or
     colour to the story.

3   Avoid adverbs such as 'wryly' to signal jokes. Do not write:

> John Smith describes himself wryly as a plain man in a million.

If the joke is good enough, the reader will not need to be nudged; if it is not, the nudging makes the joke fall flatter.

8
Style

Style differs from grammar in that it cannot be quantified: it has no precise rules. Style is concerned not so much with the mechanics of language as with the way the writer uses it to play on the sensations of the reader. Style adds impact to writing, strengthens the contact with the reader and heightens their awareness. This is true even though the reader may be unaware of what is happening and unable to analyse the techniques used.

To be effective, a journalist must develop a style that has four principal attributes: suitability, simplicity, precision and poise.

Suitability

The way a story is written must match the subject, the mood and pace of the events described and, above all, the needs of the reader. The style must arouse their interest and maintain it throughout. It must also present the facts or arguments in a way that enables the reader to understand them quickly and easily. For example:

1   If the subject is serious, treat it seriously.

2   If the subject is light, treat it lightly – for example, use a delayed-drop intro or a punning headline.

3   Whatever the subject, do not needlessly offend the reader. Thus, where a story concerns eccentric beliefs or practices, avoid cynicism and facetiousness.

4   Where a story concerns events that have action and movement, the style should suggest pace. Write tersely; avoid superfluous

adjectives and adverbs; use direct, active verbs; construct crisp, taut sentences.

5   Where a story concerns a sequence of events, a straightforward narrative style may be the best bet. If you use one event to create impact in the intro, remember to repeat the reference in its proper time context. Also, make sure your tenses are consistent.

6   Where a story concerns stark, horrific events, avoid the temptation to overwrite. The events themselves will provide all the impact you need.

7   Whatever the story, don't rhapsodise. Remember that understatement is usually more effective than overstatement.

Simplicity

Be direct: get to the point. For example:

1   Prefer the short, Anglo-Saxon word to the long, Latinate one.

2   Prefer the concrete statement to the abstract one.

3   Prefer the direct statement to any form of circumlocution.

4   Avoid words or phrases that merely sound good.

5   Avoid pomposity at all costs.

6   Remember that a sentence must have at least one verb – and that this is its most important word.

7   In general, use transitive verbs in the active voice:

Jones told the meeting he was resigning.

8   Choose adjectives with care and don't use too many. Avoid tautology: 'a *new* innovation'.

9   In general, prefer the short sentence to the long one, particularly in the intro.

10   Avoid over-complex sentences full of subordinate clauses and phrases.

Precision

Precision is vital to the journalist, above all in news reporting. To be precise you need to know exactly what words mean. Study words and their meanings and never use a word you are not sure about. Read Chapter 9, **Words**, carefully and then refer to it when necessary.

You must also master the principles of grammar to ensure that you express your meaning clearly and accurately. Read the chapters on grammar carefully and then refer to them when necessary.

As a writer, do not leave it to the sub to spot inaccuracy or ambiguity. Read your own copy and ask: 'Do I mean what I say and have I said what I mean?' Often the honest answer will be: 'No.'

If you pass that self-imposed test, ask: 'So what?' Often you will find that the story does not go far enough in saying what happens next. Remember that the reader needs to know precisely what is happening.

As a sub, always check when you rewrite that you haven't introduced new errors into the copy. And be careful when you write news headlines to fit. If your first effort is the wrong length, you will try to substitute one word for another. But a synonym must be exact or it may change the meaning of the headline. Always ask yourself finally: 'Does the headline tell the story?' If the answer is 'No', it will need further rewriting.

Also, be careful with verbs where the active and passive take the same form:

PEER OWED £20,000

This is ambiguous: was he owed the money or did he owe it?

Poise

Poise is the essence of style: it gives writing balance, ease of manner and lack of strain. Individual words should fit the context. Sentences should be a pleasure to read because they are balanced and rhythmical. Paragraphs should be written to convey the writer's meaning and leave the reader in no doubt that they have grasped it.

With the best prose the reader remains unconscious of technique: they simply enjoy reading the passage. The hard work should all be done by the writer (with a bit of polish by the sub).

Study the section on stylistic devices that follows. Practise using them where appropriate. But, above all, look for good models in journalism and writing generally. If a piece of prose excites you, study it, analyse it – even imitate it. Do not be too proud to copy other writers' tricks.

Stylistic devices

Most of the stylistic devices that follow are called tropes or figures of speech. There is no reason why you should learn the names of the more obscure ones, such as synecdoche or metonymy. We take both of these for granted. What could be more natural than to say 'All hands on deck' (synecdoche) or 'He is a lover of the bottle' (metonymy)? But it is worth remembering that they are in fact figures of speech.

Alliteration

Alliteration is the repetition of an initial sound in words that follow each other:

> Sing a song of sixpence

Use in light-hearted stories, particularly in headlines. Do not use in serious stories.

Assonance

Assonance is the repetition of a vowel sound in words that follow each other:

> The cat sat on my lap.

Use in light-hearted stories, particularly in headlines. Do not use in serious stories.

Graveyard (also black, gallows, sick) humour

This is making jokes about such things as injury, disease, disability and death. It is an understandable reaction by journalists (also police officers, soldiers, doctors, nurses and others) to the hard facts of life and death.

Enjoy the jokes but do not let them get into print. The headline 'Hot under the cholera' once appeared over a story about an epidemic. This is also an example of the compulsive pun.

Hyperbole

Hyperbole is extravagant and obvious exaggeration:

   a million thanks

Of all figures of speech, hyperbole is the most used – and abused – by journalists. Handle with care.

Irony

Irony is either making a point in words that mean literally the opposite or a condition in which a person seems mocked by fate or the facts.

A story about a woman who survives a car crash, borrows a mobile phone and telephones her husband to report her survival – only to be knocked down and killed a moment later – is an example of irony.

In this example telling the story is enough: we do not need to be reminded that it is irony.

Use the word 'irony' sparingly. In particular, avoid the adverb 'ironically', which is usually a lazy way of trying to make a surprise sound more significant than it is.

Litotes

Litotes is the opposite of hyperbole. It is understatement, especially assertion by negation of the contrary. Instead of 'Rome is a great city':

   Rome is no mean city.

Metaphor

Metaphor is calling something by the name of what it resembles:

> To suffer the slings and arrows of outrageous fortune . . .

Frequent repetition of metaphors turns them into clichés (see Chapter 9, **Words**). Careless use of metaphors can lead to the mixed metaphor, an expression in which two or more metaphors are confused:

> to take arms against a sea of troubles
>
> (you wouldn't use *weapons* to fight the *waves*)

The fact that Shakespeare did it is no defence: Hamlet was mad. So avoid the mixed metaphor at all costs since it has the opposite effect of that intended. Instead of making your prose vivid it produces the effect of absurdity.

Metonymy

Metonymy is replacing the name of something by the name of a related thing:

> He is a lover of the bottle [instead of drink].

Onomatopoeia

Onomatopoeia is using words whose sound helps to suggest the meaning:

> He has a hacking cough.

Oxymoron

Oxymoron is combining contradictory terms to form an expressive phrase:

> He shows cruel kindness.

Pun

A pun is a play on words alike or nearly alike in sound but different in meaning:

ALL THE FAX ABOUT NEW TECHNOLOGY

The pun is overused by headline-writers who can't break the habit. *Never use a pun over a serious story.*

A subtler form of word play recycles an old meaning:

ARE YOU A VIRGIN ABOUT OLIVE OIL?

Repetition

Repetition on purpose emphasises:

O Romeo, Romeo! Wherefore art thou Romeo?

In general, prefer repetition to variation.

Rhetoric

Rhetoric is a general term for the art of using language to persuade or impress others. Note particularly the rhetorical question that journalists address to their readers:

Have you ever been to China?

Use in chatty features, but rarely elsewhere.

Simile

Simile is likening something to something else:

My love is like a red, red rose . . .

Frequent repetition of similes turns them into clichés (see Chapter 9, **Words**) – avoid this like the plague.

Synecdoche

Synecdoche is using the part for the whole or the whole for the part:

All hands on deck.

Variation

Variation is using a different word or phrase to describe something in order to avoid repetition and/or to add colour to the copy. When done to impress it is called 'elegant variation':

Instead of talking about a *spade* I shall from now on refer to a *horticultural implement*.

This kind of variation is a bad idea because what results is at least strained and sometimes ludicrous.

More common is the variation that tries to avoid repetition:

Northern Ireland has a higher rate of unemployment than at any other time in the *province's* history.

Before using this kind of variation ask yourself the following questions:

1   Would a pronoun do as well? In the example above 'its' could easily replace 'the province's'.

2   Is the variation word/phrase an exact equivalent? (Here the province of Ulster has three counties in the Irish Republic.)

3   Is the variation necessary or could you avoid it by rewriting the sentence?

4   Would repetition have as much impact as variation?

The need to repeat or vary words is often a clue to bad structure. For example, where an intro doubles back on itself, it should be rewritten. Where you are tempted to use 'however' because you have just used 'but', you are making the reader work too hard.

9
Words

Precision and effectiveness in writing depend on the careful use of language. You must learn to recognise the words and phrases that will convey your meaning exactly and vividly to the reader. And you must reject any word or phrase that is flabby and worn out.

The development of word power comes only with practice. Besides a sensitivity to language it demands an inquiring mind and a careful attitude. You must avoid careless mistakes and also be concerned about quality, taking professional pride in your skill as a writer.

This attitude cannot be taught, only caught. But it is worth pointing out common pitfalls.

Exaggeration

Many errors occur because the writer overstates the case in an effort to achieve impact: this is perhaps the journalist's most common fault. It is this striving for effect that makes every rescuer 'a hero', every disturbance a 'fracas', every confusion a 'chaos' and every fire an 'inferno' (the word means hell).

Here the advice must be: never use a word whose meaning you are unsure about; always check the dictionary definition and derivation of an unfamiliar word.

Tabloidese

The search for a short word to use in a headline has created a specialised subs' vocabulary that, on some papers, turns every investigation into a 'probe', every attempt into a 'bid' and every disagreement into a 'row'.

It would be perverse to object to the use of these words in headlines, although a succession of them reads like parody. A sub who writes:

VICE VICAR TELLS ALL IN PROBE BID ROW

is clearly overdoing it.

The real problem comes when this essentially made-up language creeps into the text. Such words as 'rap', 'slam' and 'axe' litter the pages of the downmarket tabloids. As Keith Waterhouse has pointed out, the objection to these words is that people don't use them in everyday speech.

> Why, if these words are now so common, are they not in common use? Why do we not hear housewives at bus-stops saying . . . 'Did I tell you about young Fred being rapped after he slammed his boss? He thinks he's going to be axed'?
> (Keith Waterhouse, *Waterhouse on Newspaper Style*, Viking, 1989 pp. 229–30)

So think hard before using the following words in text:

aid	(help)	brand	(describe)
aim	(intend)	bungle	(mistake)
alert	(tell)		
axe	(sack)	call	(propose)
		chief	(leader)
ban	(prohibit, exclude)	clampdown	(control)
bar	(exclude)	clash	(dispute)
battle	(dispute)	condemn	(criticise)
bid	(try, attempt)	crackdown	(control)
blast	(criticise)	crusade	(campaign)
blaze	(fire)	curb	(restrict)
blitz	(drive)	curse	(bad luck)
blow	(disappointment)		
blunder	(mistake)	dash	(hurry)
bombshell	(unexpected event)	deal	(agreement, arrangement)
boob	(mistake, breast)	don	(put on)
boost	(encourage, increase)	drama	(event)
		dramatic	(unusual)
boot out	(expel)	dub	(describe)

dump	(sack)	quit	(resign)
dwell	(live)	quiz	(question)
epic	(very unusual)	race	(hurry)
		rally	(support)
face	(expect)	rap	(tell off)
feud	(quarrel)	rebel	(person
fury	(anger)		disagreeing)
		riddle	(mystery)
grab	(take)	rock	(shock)
		romp	(sex, have sex)
headache	(problem)	row	(dispute)
hike	(increase)	rumpus	(dispute)
hit out	(criticise)		
hurdle	(difficulty)	scrap	(cancel)
		set to	(likely to)
inferno	(fire)	shake-up	(reform)
		shock	(surprise)
jinx	(bad luck)	shun	(avoid)
		slam	(criticise)
kick out	(expel)	slap	(impose)
		slash	(reduce)
launch	(start)	snag	(difficulty)
loom	(threaten)	snub	(fail to attend)
		soar	(increase)
mercy	(relief)	storm out	(resign)
		swoop	(raid)
oust	(replace)		
outrage	(anger)	threat	(possibility)
peace	(end to dispute)	unveil	(announce)
plan	(proposal)		
pledge	(promise)	vice	(sex)
plunge	(fall)	vigil	(patrol)
poised	(ready)	vow	(promise)
probe	(inquiry)		
		war	(rivalry)

Posh words

Posh, pompous, pretentious words are the opposite of tabloidese: they show the writer putting on collar and tie to impress. Many posh words used in journalism are also examples of circumlocution (long-winded and roundabout writing) or euphemism (using a mild-sounding alternative word to avoid giving offence). In general, prefer plain words to posh ones. For example, avoid:

a large proportion of	(much of)
accede to	(allow, grant)
accommodate	(hold)
accordingly	(so)
additionally	(also)
address	(face, approach)
adjacent to	(near, next to)
ameliorate	(improve)
amidst	(amid)
amongst	(among)
approximately	(about)
ascertain	(learn)
assist/ance	(help)
at an early date	(soon)
at present/ at the present time	(now)
attempt	(try)
beverage	(drink)
commence	(begin, start)
concept	(idea)
concerning	(about)
construct	(build, make)
converse	(talk)
customary	(usual)
deceased	(dead)
demise	(death)
demonstrate	(show)
dentures	(false teeth)
despite	(although)
discontinue	(stop)
dispatch	(send)
donate	(give)
draw to the attention of	(point out)
dwell	(live)
edifice	(building)
endeavour	(try)
eventuate	(happen)
evince	(show)
exceedingly	(very)
expedite	(hurry)
extremely	(very)
facilitate	(ease, help)
finalise	(complete)
following	(after)
frequently	(often)
give rise to	(cause)
implement	(carry out)
in addition	(also)
in addition to	(as well as)
in attendance	(present)
in conjunction with	(and)
in consequence of	(because)
indicate	(show, point, point out, say, imply)
in excess of	(more than)
inform	(tell)
initiate	(begin, start)
in order to	(to)
inquire	(ask)
in short supply	(scarce)
in spite of the fact that	(although)

in the course of	(during)	previous	(earlier)
in the event of	(if)	prior to	(before)
in the neigh-bourhood/vicinity of	(near)	proceed	(go)
		purchase	(buy)
in the region of	(about)	regarding	(about)
in view of the fact that	(since)	remunerate	(pay)
		require	(need)
		residence	(home)
less expensive	(cheaper)	resuscitate	(revive)
locate	(find)		
location	(place)	somewhat	(rather)
		subsequently	(later)
made good their escape	(escaped)	sufficient	(enough)
manufacture	(make)	terminate	(end)
missive	(letter)	to date	(so far)
		transportation	(transport)
necessitate	(compel)		
nevertheless	(but)	upon	(on)
nonetheless	(but)	utilise	(use)
objective	(aim)	venue	(place)
of the order of	(about)		
on the part of	(by)	was of the opinion that	(thought)
owing to the fact that	(because)	was suffering from	(had)
pass away/over/to the other side	(die)	when and if	(if)
		whilst	(while)
		with the exception of	(except)
personnel	(workers)		

The word 'dwell' contrives to be both tabloidese and posh: a double reason for not using it. The word 'indicate' is a particular trap: does it mean show, point, point out, say or imply? If it's precision you want, avoid 'indicate' altogether. Envelopes are addressed, and golf balls, but not problems – except by the pretentious.

Vogue words

Some (usually long) words become fashionable. Suddenly they are every-where – used with meaningless frequency by journalists who are keen to be considered smart or who are too idle to develop their own vocabulary.

Using a phrase such as 'the eponymous protagonist' to describe Hamlet is almost always a sign of showing off. So take care with the following:

agenda	dichotomy	insulate	replete
ambience	dilemma		
ambivalent		meaningful	seminal
archetypal	egregious	meritocracy	symbiosis
axiomatic	emotive	milieu	syndrome
	empathy	mores	
cachet	eponymous		technocrat
catalyst	escalate	parameter	
charisma	exponential	pragmatism	vertiginous
conceptual		protagonist	viable
coterie	iconic	purposive	vicarious

If you are tempted to use one of these words ask yourself:

1   Is it the exact word you need?

2   Is there an alternative that would be as accurate – and more comprehensible?

3   If not, can the word be understood from its context, or does it need some qualification to help the reader? (If it does then perhaps it is not the right word.)

Jargon

Jargon is specialised vocabulary, familiar to the members of a group, trade or profession. If you write for a newspaper or general magazine you should try to translate jargon into ordinary English whenever you can. If you write for a specialist magazine there is a stronger case for leaving some terms as they are, but you must be sure that the reader will understand them.

A common source of jargon is scientific, medical, government and legal handouts. Avoid such examples of officialese as:

ambulatory patient	(one that has been allowed up)
domiciliary unit	(home)
hospitalised	(sent to hospital)

There are also ugly words in industry, but you cannot always avoid them. 'Containerisation', for example, has a precise meaning and is difficult to translate.

'Redundancy' may appear to be a euphemism for sacking – but there is a big difference between the two terms. A person made redundant will not be replaced: their job has been abolished. A person sacked is likely to be replaced.

'Packing' is not the same as 'packaging'; 'marketing' is not the same as 'selling'; 'targeting' may be an ugly word but it is what sales and marketing people say they do when they set out to identify and capture a market. So use these terms where necessary in context but do not use them in general stories.

The computer industry has spawned its own ugly terminology – answer-back, boot up, end-user, formatted, throughput, input, hardware, software. It is apt for that industry since it conveys particular, precise meanings to those who work with computers.

But journalists (except those on computer magazines) should avoid such terms as 'throughput'. We already have words to describe these ideas. They may be less trendy but they are at least as clear as computer jargon and certainly more elegant.

Slang

'Write as you speak' can be good general advice. Better by far the vigour and freshness of the spoken word than the dull formality of the official report or the business letter.

But be careful with slang, which could be called the jargon of the street. Similar arguments apply here. Will the reader understand it? Is it ugly? Has the word become accepted?

And does it fit the context? You would not use slang in reporting the mayor's funeral – but you might well use jazz slang in writing a colour piece on Dizzy Gillespie's funeral.

Be particularly careful with rhyming slang, which can be euphemistic:

berk	(Berkeley Hunt – cunt)
bottle	(and glass – arse)
bristols	(Bristol Cities – titties)
cobblers	(cobblers' awls – balls)

Euphemism

In general, avoid euphemism: call a spade a spade. 'Manhood' is a comical way of referring to the penis and 'sleeping with' a prostitute unlikely.

Four-letter words . . .

. . . including of course swear words with more than four letters. Should you use them in copy? And if so, should they be printed in full or muffled by asterisks?

Essentially this is a matter of editorial policy and style. When in doubt, check with your editor or department head.

But it's worth noting that there are far more swear words than there used to be – in journalism as in ordinary conversation. And that tabloids are more likely than broadsheets to protect their readers' sensibilities by asterisks.

Words with two possible meanings

With some words the problem is that they mean different things to different people. To the history don, for example, a 'chauvinist' is an aggressive patriot, a flag-waver, while to almost anyone under 60 a chauvinist is somebody who puts women down.

Below are some examples of words that can cause confusion. So use them with care – if in doubt, find an alternative.

Note: in most cases the first meaning given is the earlier, 'correct' one, even though the later, looser one may now be more common. (See also **Confusing pairs**, overleaf.)

aggravate:	1 make worse; 2 annoy
alibi:	1 evidence that the accused was elsewhere when a crime was being committed; 2 excuse
anticipate:	1 use, spend, deal with in advance; 2 expect
arguably:	1 possibly; 2 probably
celibate:	1 unmarried; 2 abstaining from sex
chauvinist:	1 absurdly nationalistic; 2 sexist
chronic:	1 lingering, recurrent; 2 very bad, severe
cleave:	1 split; 2 stick
cohort:	1 group of people (originally military); 2 individual colleague or assistant
contemporary:	1 belonging to the same time; 2 modern
decimate:	1 kill one in ten; 2 kill or destroy large numbers
dilemma:	1 choice between two equally unwelcome possibilities; 2 awkward problem
egregious:	1 distinguished; 2 notorious
fulsome:	1 excessive; 2 copious
gay:	1 light-hearted; 2 homosexual
geriatric:	1 relating to care of the old; 2 old
pristine:	1 original, former; 2 new, fresh, pure
protagonist:	1 chief actor; 2 any participant
refute:	1 show to be false; 2 contradict, deny
regularly:	1 at regular intervals; 2 often
scan:	1 examine closely; 2 glance at (also of verse to conform to rules of metre)
shambles:	1 slaughterhouse; 2 confusion

Confusing pairs

There are many pairs of words in English that sound similar and are often confused. The pitfall here is not that the two words are thought to have the same meaning but that the unwary writer uses one by mistake for the other – and thus produces an entirely different meaning. In some cases (such as the trio 'assure/ensure/insure') each word has gradually acquired its own distinct meaning: they all mean 'make sure' but in different ways.

See also Chapter 5, **Spelling**, for pairs of words that sound identical and are often confused.

abrogate	(abolish)
arrogate	(claim presumptuously)
affect	(influence, adopt)
effect	(as verb, accomplish)
appraise	(determine the value of)
apprise	(inform)
assure	(give confidence to)
ensure	(make happen)
insure	(arrange insurance)
barbaric	(crude, uncivilised)
barbarous	(cruel)
censor	(prevent publication)
censure	(criticise harshly)
chafe	(make sore)
chaff	(tease)
complacent	(smug)
complaisant	(obliging)
comprehensive	(exhaustive)
comprehensible	(intelligible)
contemptible	(deserving contempt)
contemptuous	(showing contempt)
continual	(recurring with breaks)
continuous	(without a break)
credible	(believable)
credulous	(believing too easily)
defective	(damaged)
deficient	(short of)
definite	(precise)
definitive	(conclusive)
deprecate	(argue or protest against)
depreciate	(fall in value)
derisive	(showing contempt)
derisory	(deserving contempt)

disinterested	(impartial)
uninterested	(bored)
economic	(of economics, enough to give a good return)
economical	(thrifty)
elemental	(basic)
elementary	(simple)
eligible	(suitable)
illegible	(unclear)
equable	(steady)
equitable	(fair)
evolve	(develop)
devolve	(hand down)
evince	(show)
evoke	(draw out)
exhaustive	(comprehensive)
exhausted	(tired)
exigent	(urgent)
exiguous	(scanty)
explicit	(stated in detail)
implicit	(implied)
farther	(used of distance only)
further	(used of quantity and distance)
flaunt	(display ostentatiously)
flout	(treat with contempt)
forceful	(energetic)
forcible	(done by force)
fortuitous	(accidental)
fortunate	(lucky)
historic	(famous in history)
historical	(belonging to history)
imply	(suggest)
infer	(deduce)
inchoate	(rudimentary)
incoherent	(disjointed)
ingenious	(cleverly contrived)
ingenuous	(frank)

intense	(extreme)
intensive	(concentrated)
loath/loth	(unwilling)
loathe	(detest)
luxuriant	(profuse)
luxurious	(opulent)
masterful	(dominating)
masterly	(skilful)
militate	(contend)
mitigate	(soften)
oral	(spoken)
verbal	(of words, written or spoken)
ordinance	(decree)
ordnance	(arrangement, usually military)
partly	(in part)
partially	(incompletely)
politic	(prudent)
political	(of politics)
practical	(opposite of theoretical)
practicable	(capable of being done)
prescribe	(lay down)
proscribe	(prohibit)
prevaricate	(evade the truth)
procrastinate	(defer action)
prostate	(gland)
prostrate	(lying)
reluctant	(unwilling)
reticent	(reluctant to speak)
repel	(offend)
repulse	(drive back)
sensual	(physical, gratifying to the body)
sensuous	(affecting or appealing to the senses, especially by beauty or delicacy)
titillate	(tease, arouse)
titivate	(smarten)

tortuous	(winding)
torturous	(causing torture)
venal	(corruptible)
venial	(excusable)

Redundant words

Many words used are superfluous, for example adjectives ('*true* facts'), prepositions ('fill *up* a bottle') or phrases ('for *the month of* January'). Often a writer feels the need to add a redundant word or phrase because they do not know the meaning of a particular word. Never do this. Always check what a word means, then decide whether your reader will understand it – without the redundant addition. Here are some examples to avoid:

appreciate *in value*
chief protagonist
close scrutiny
completely surround
comprise *of*
consensus *of opinion*
cut *back*
free gift
general consensus
in *actual* fact
revert *back*
temporary respite
total annihilation
self-confessed

Many redundant expressions trip off the tongue – or can be found in legal documents. But in copy avoid:

aid and abet
each and every
first and foremost
(without) let or hindrance
neat and tidy
null and void
ways and means

See also **Saying it twice**, pp. 28–9.

Non-existent words

By all means make up a word if the context demands it. But avoid making up non-existent words by mistake. Do not run together words that belong apart or add syllables to words that do not need them. For example use:

a lot *not* alot
dissociate *not* disassociate
preventive *not* preventative
recur *not* reoccur

'Alright' is now all right in some publications – as always, check your house style. Also note: 'adaptation' *not* 'adaption'.

Empty words

Some words are, simply, empty. 'Simply' used like this is one of them. So is 'basically'. They tend to be used in speech as an alternative to 'er' to give the speaker thinking time. Avoid them in writing unless in quoting somebody you wish to give the impression that they are empty headed. For example:

at the end of the day
basically
by and large
currently
I mean
meaningful
simply
you know
well

Americanisms

American is not a foreign language but a dialect (or series of dialects) of English. And to it we owe much of the vigour of modern English prose. Without writers such as Hemingway our language would be a tired, anaemic thing. American expressions are everywhere. Some enrich the language by saying something previously unsaid or by providing a direct or vivid alternative to the ordinary British expression. The American 'muffler', for example, is a more precise word for 'silencer'.

Others are ugly, clumsy and pointless. Then there are those that make sense to Americans – but if they mean anything at all in Britain, mean something else.

And the position is constantly changing. Yesterday's Americanism, like yesterday's slang, can turn into today's standard English.

Thus British children are increasingly being 'raised' rather than 'brought up': the American expression is shorter, more direct – no problem. But Britons still ask for a 'rise' in salary rather than a 'raise'. And 'hike', though shorter than 'increase', still suggests fit young people in shorts striding through the countryside.

In British press reports of the 1996 French transport dispute 'truckers' kept appearing. Again, no problem: the word is shorter than 'truck/lorry driver' and clear. But a British headline about 'vets' (for 'army veterans') inspired a reader's letter pointing out that in Britain 'vets' were 'veterinary surgeons'.

And there is a problem about the use of the picturesque American word 'seafood'. Over here it is used to mean either 'shellfish' or 'fish *and* shellfish' – to the gourmand an important distinction.

So be careful in your use of American imports. Above all, avoid those that turn a noun into a verb when a perfectly good verb already exists and those that lengthen an expression without adding to it. For example, do not use:

to consult with	(for) (to consult)
to gift	(to give)
to loan	(to lend)
transportation	(transport)
utilisation	(use)

But what's the main difference between 'envisage' and 'envision', say? The first is British and the second American. If you work for *Time Out* – a magazine whose title proclaims it as under American influence – there probably won't be a problem. Otherwise there often will be: remember your reader.

Clichés

Everybody who advises on writing in general and journalism in particular says you must avoid clichés. And you must certainly try to avoid the hilarious/embarrassing ones listed below. But a certain amount of formula-writing, in both structure and vocabulary, is inevitable in routine journalism, whether it is a news story or a piece of instructional copy. A worse fault is to try so hard to be original that you end up sounding pretentious.

And there is of course a worse mistake than using a cliché: misusing one. Do not write 'He is as deaf as a doornail' or 'She is as dead as a post.' Avoid mixing two clichés together. Do not write: 'I am full of nothing but praise.' This runs together into a nonsensical cocktail the two stock phrases 'I am full of (praise)' and 'I have nothing but (praise).'

Some common expressions are almost always misused. For example, 'to beg the question' does not mean 'to raise the question' but to avoid the question and so to use as the basis of proof something that itself needs proving. It means arguing in a circle.

A leading question in law is a question put in such a way as to suggest the desired answer. It is helpful rather than hostile.

'The exception proves the rule' means that the exception tests the rule (from the original meaning of 'prove', which also gives us the page proof and that other phrase 'the proof of the pudding is in the eating'), and in law that the making of an exception proves that the rule holds *in cases not excepted.* Thus a notice saying 'Today students may leave early' implies that they usually have to stay late.

The expression cannot mean that an exception to the rule makes it valid.

If you find these definitions difficult to follow – or remember – the best advice may be to avoid the expressions altogether.

If you do use a cliché, don't apologise for doing so by using another one. The following expressions are all lame apologies:

> to coin a phrase (always used ironically)
>
> as the saying goes/as the old joke has it
>
> the proverbial . . . (avoid this even if a proverb is quoted)

the *Times* online style book includes the following list of clichés, saying they should be 'resisted strongly in almost every context':

> backlash, basically, beleaguered, blueprint, bombshell, bonanza, brainchild, chaos, charisma, clampdown, consensus, crackdown, crisis, crunch, drama/dramatic, escalate, facelift, gunned down, hopefully, ironically, legendary, major, massive, mega-, nightmare, prestigious, quantum leap, reportedly, shambles, shock, shoot-out, situation, trauma/traumatic, unique.

Only two of these words, 'major' and 'massive', also crop up in the *Guardian's* equivalent list of 'overused words and phrases to be avoided'. The others are:

> back burner, boost (massive or otherwise), bouquets and brickbats, but hey . . ., drop-dead gorgeous, insisted, luvvies, political correctness, politically correct, PC, raft of measures, special, to die for, upsurge (surge will do).

The *Guardian* style book also quotes a survey by the Plain English Campaign which found that the most irritating phrase in the language was 'at the end of the day', followed by (in order of annoyance):

> at this moment in time, like (as in, like, this), with all due respect, to be perfectly honest with you, touch base, I hear what you're saying, going forward, absolutely, blue-sky thinking.

Other words and phrases that upset people included:

> 24/7, ballpark figure, bottom line, diamond geezer, it's not rocket science, ongoing, prioritise, pushing the envelope, singing from the same hymn sheet, thinking outside the box.

Every area of journalism has its own set of clichés to be avoided by careful writers and subs. Here, for example, is the *Times Literary Supplement's* list of 20 words and phrases to be cut from book reviews:

1   mordant wit
2   If (so-and-so) didn't, exist, it/he/she would have to be invented
3   rich tapestry
4   . . . a hilarious and searing indictment of Britain today
5   smorgasbord (of ideas)

6   consummate (as in 'consummate skill')
7   surfing (metaphorically)
8   eponymous (as in 'the eponymous hero')
9   feisty
10   in spite of (or perhaps because of) etc
11   he/she writes like an angel
12   this curate's egg (of a book)
13   peppered with
14   baggy monster (of a novel)
15   . . . but (such-and-such) looks like carelessness
16   these are mere cavils, minor quibbles, etc
17   (such-and-such/so-and-so) is that rare thing, a . . .
18   made me laugh out loud, couldn't put it down (etc)
19   having said that . . . arguably . . . (etc)
20   . . . reminds one of Martin Amis.

Misquotations and factual mistakes

Journalists should know what they are talking about. And when they quote, whether it is the people they interview or the books they read, they should quote accurately. For example, it isn't 'a little knowledge' that is said to be a dangerous thing but 'a little learning'. So also:

Nor all, that *glisters* [not 'glitters'], gold.

To gild refined gold, to *paint* the lily [not 'to gild the lily'].

Till death *us do* [not 'do us'] part.

Water, water everywhere *nor any* [not 'and not a'] drop to drink.

The 'mother of Parliaments' is not the House of Commons but England. And Humphrey Bogart in *Casablanca* never says: 'Play it again, Sam.'

As Bill Bryson has pointed out, the ship whose crew famously disappeared was the *Mary*, not Marie, *Celeste* and Hobson's choice (the horse by the stable door) is not a difficult one but no choice at all.

Frankenstein was not the monster in Mary Shelley's novel but the monster's creator.

Billy the Kid was not left-handed. That belief arose because a famous photograph of him was reversed when it was reproduced, making it look as though he wore his holster on the left.

And finally journalists almost always get the King Canute story wrong. When he told the tide to stop coming in he was not arrogantly expecting it to obey him; by contrast he was showing his courtiers that he was not omnipotent.

Here, as everywhere, the moral is: if you want to be sure, get hold of a reference book and check.

Mistakes

'Accrue' is confused with 'acquire':

> Nearly a year after Hanan Saleh Matrud's death, her family have accrued a small pile of documents that tell of a young girl's life hardly lived. (news story)

'Address' is a vogue word, here used instead of 'answer':

> This was also a race which went a long way towards addressing those critics of formula one who claim that the sport offers insufficient genuine overtaking on the circuit. (motor-racing report)

'Akimbo' technically refers to arms, not legs, being wide apart:

> After years of keeping us legs akimbo in the lithotomy position, our rulers now want us to jump down and push. (feature)

'Altercation' is verbal, not physical:

> Lehmann let Spurs equalise in stoppage time when he became involved in an altercation [in fact a shove] with Robbie Keane, who converted the penalty.

'Anticipate' is a pompous way of saying 'expect' (here used for variation):

> Jenson Button did not expect to be battling for second place in the German grand prix any more than he anticipated having to drive one-handed for the last 20 laps . . . (motor-racing report)

'Careen' is confused with 'career':

> Howard careens off again, first to a pub, then to Carlene's wake. (book review)

'Chronic' can be confusing if used to mean very bad:

> It was just such bad television, such a chronic mistiming of mood and emphasis. (TV review)

'Coin' means 'invent' – but it can't mean that here:

> To coin one of Arnold Schwarzenegger's best-known and over-used lines: 'Hasta la vista, baby.' (news story)

'Coruscate' (sparkle) is confused with 'excoriate' (criticise severely):

> Jonathon Porritt mounts a coruscating attack on the UK environment movement for its lack of effectiveness. (feature)

'Decimate' (originally kill one in ten, nowadays often destroy) conveys confusion rather than clarity:

> After the more-than-decimating visits of King Death, minds did change, in subtle but inwardly seismic ways. (book review)

> Whales used to appear in the Thames reasonably often in the days before industrial whaling decimated their populations. (feature)

> The cattle and camel-herding communities who live there are too poor to buy food in the marketplace when their herds are decimated by drought. (news story)

> The Soviets did not shuffle populations for the same reasons as the Nazis . . . there is a subtle difference between decimation and annihilation. (book review)

> [New Labour] swept into office with one of the grandest majorities of all time. Its weary old Tory predecessor was decimated. (feature)

'Demise', a pompous word for death, shouldn't be used for 'fall', still less 'decline':

> In all the excitement over Mr Tony Blair's demise, the one I feel sorry for is Alan Milburn. (diary)

'Dilemma' only has point as a word when it means something more than problem (difficult choice between two courses of action); as an alternative to 'problem' it is just pretentious:

'Where did I leave the car keys? [etc] . . .' All these dilemmas will be familiar to anyone over 50. (column)

'Discern' is confused with 'distinguish':

'This movie fails to discern between those who murder innocent civilians in their sleep and those who hunt down the murderers.' (feature)

'Disinterest(ed)' is confused with 'lack of interest, uninterested':

Hunched in a chair in his publicist's office, he talks for a bit and then peters out, averting his eyes and sinking into himself with flinty disinterest. (feature)

'Diurnal' is not, like 'quotidian', a literary alternative to 'daily'; it means by day rather than by night (the opposite of 'nocturnal'), whereas here the writer intends 'daily':

We are asked to believe that the Queen Vic pub, East End boozer of diurnal punch-ups, holds Diwali celebrations. (feature)

'Divest (yourself)' is 'undress, free, get rid', not 'express':

He later divested himself of various antediluvian views about women, homosexuals and Ulster. (feature)

'Egregious' (outstanding) can be confusing because it is usually negative, though sometimes positive:

The shooting of Menezes, wrongly mistaken for a suicide bomber at Stockwell tube station, a disaster that seems more egregious with every newly leaked detail. (feature)

Banville is, as I observe him, an egregiously modest writer. (feature)

'Enhance' is a positive word, here confused with 'aggravate' (make worse):

To do otherwise is to risk enhancing the injury. (feature)

'Equitable' is confused with 'equable':

'One of the demands of leadership is keeping your head and, I hope, your equitable temperament.' (feature)

'Eschew' is a literary word for 'avoid, shun' – it doesn't mean 'oppose':

> Perhaps some of the Labour electorate eschew both Blair and Brown
> as prime minister. (reader's letter)

'Forcibly' means 'by physical force' – did Mrs T literally handbag Ken?

> This precious London land was sold to the community for peanuts the
> day before Ken Livingstone was forcibly removed from County Hall by
> Mrs Thatcher in 1986. (feature)

'Fulsome' can be confusing because it is either positive ('abundant, full')
or negative ('over-abundant, excessive'):

> The speaker at the memorial meeting will be suitably fulsome about
> our virtues and discreet about our vices. (column)

'Gender' and 'sex' can be useful alternatives as words ('gender' now
usually means sexual difference); they should not be used in the same
sentence to mean the same thing:

> People who are determined to get the gender of baby they want can
> often find a doctor to perform an abortion on a foetus of the wrong
> sex, illegal though it is. (feature)

'Genocide' (the killing of an ethnic group) is a powerful word that should
be kept for people:

> Off northern Scotland, birds and fish are suffering from the near
> genocide of the sand-eels they eat, taken by netsmen for fishmeal.
> (feature)

'Heyday' exists only in the singular – 'the heyday':

> The 1970s, remember, were one of the heydays of British playwriting.
> (feature)

'Historical' is confused with 'historic':

> The only way forward is for these two ancient rivals to find a historical
> compromise. (feature)

'Hospitalise' is an ugly way of saying 'in hospital' or 'beaten up':

> He would, though, still have been hospitalised at the time of a leadership contest. (feature)

> Children being hospitalised by school bullies, presumably for being a bit different. (feature)

'Inchoate(ly)' is confused with 'incoherent(ly)':

> The film-maker maunders about inchoately in the documentary, showing a 'different' slice of life. (feature)

> I tried to ignore a certain inchoate emotion that I couldn't quite place. It was a vague emotion, fuzzy but not warm. (feature)

'Infer' is confused with 'imply':

> In fact, said Lord Deedes in the *Daily Telegraph*, [*Private Eye*'s Dear Bill] column was politically useful. 'It made it difficult to seriously infer that Denis had the smallest influence on his wife's policies.' (feature)

'Liaison' means relationship not 'encounter':

> The killer was enjoying sexual liaisons with someone other than his wife. (feature)

'Literally' can only be used to say that a metaphorical phrase is not, in fact, a metaphor:

> Spinoza was born in the prosperous city of Amsterdam in 1632, literally in the middle of Holland's golden age. (feature)

This doesn't work because 'in the middle of Holland's golden age' can only mean what it says. (The writer wants something like 'plumb'.)

> He was quite literally a man at the end of his physical and mental tether. (feature)

A 'tether' is what an animal is tied to – it can only be used metaphorically of people.

> Spitting is not in itself a violent act. It is rather a quite literally visceral means of expressing extreme contempt. (feature)

The 'viscera' is the guts – vomiting is literally visceral but spitting can't be.

> The Prince of Wales's private pilgrimage last week to Mount Athos, the Orthodox Church's most sacred site, was almost literally a trip into the past. (feature)

'Quite' is a pointless emphasis for 'literally' and 'almost' doesn't work either – something is either literally true or it isn't.

'Masterful' is confused with 'masterly':

> Julie Myerson on a masterful debut (standfirst)

'Peruse' is a pompous word for read, now creeping in elsewhere:

> As anyone who has perused Paris boutiques will know, shopping in the French capital can be a bittersweet experience. (diary)

'Pristine', which once meant original, is now a vogue word for unspoilt, in good condition:

> Once mown and rolled further, [the playing surface at Lord's] promises to be pristine at the start, with good pace and even bounce. (cricket report)

'Raze' means demolish so 'to the ground' is unnecessary:

> Three houses were razed to the ground and 22 people died. (news story)

'Rebuff' is a vogue word for deny:

> Claims that the Foreign Secretary panicked about the accession of eastern European countries to the European Union in the spring have also been rebuffed. (news story)

'Recreant' does exist as a word but it's archaic and means cowardly; here the writer probably intends 'miscreant' (scoundrel):

> Motley-Wilcock and her six colleagues [private investigators] deal with the messy and emotional world of failing relationships, small businesses with a recreant in their midst and middle-aged women targeted by debonair but ruthless conmen. (feature)

'Refute', which has the technical meaning of disprove (a claim or argument), is often used instead of 'deny':

Levy refutes that Santini left for football reasons. (feature)

That is clumsy but clear. In the next example does 'refute' mean reject or demolish the case for?

At the Labour conference in 1978, Jim Callaghan explicitly refuted demand management as a way of maintaining high employment. (feature)

'Registry' (office) is a common mistake for 'register':

In registry offices all over the land, lesbian and gay partners will, at last, gain legal recognition. (feature)

'Rehearse' is a trendy but silly alternative to 'discuss':

Questions of sexuality are endlessly rehearsed behind the closed doors of the seminar group. (feature)

'Replete' is confused with 'complete':

Book-lovers in Gosport, Hampshire, are grumbling at being turfed out of their library to make way for a refurb to create a Discovery Centre replete with coffee shop, crèche and a 'performance space'. (news story)

'Reticent' is confused with 'reluctant':

Following his exposure, Behring, however, may be more reticent to return. (news story)

'Rife' means prevalent so it can't be used of the community:

The community wrestles with poverty and is rife with drugs and gangs. (feature)

'Seeing' is a curious euphemism for having sex with (and 'falling' pregnant is not much better):

I was seeing the father of my 18-month-old baby for three months before I fell pregnant. (problem page)

'Syndrome' (cluster of medical symptoms) is a silly, pretentious word for a single problem or defect:

> What always drove Jane Fonda, of course, was the need to be seen as strenuously perfect. This is not an uncommon syndrome. (feature)

'Tortuous' (winding) is confused with 'torturous' (painful):

> David's records included tortuous personal video-diary footage: 'If you're not me, you really shouldn't be watching this.' (feature)

'Ubiquitous' (to be found everywhere) is an absolute adjective and so can't be qualified:

> Britain's most ubiquitous psychiatrist was yesterday at the centre of a plagiarism row. (news story)

'Trustee' is confused with 'trusty':

> Barry Sheerman (if he was ever a prisoner, he'd be a trustee, bringing the governor his wine and cigars) praised her for being 'clear and cool'. (feature)

'Unique' is an absolute adjective and 'uniquely' an absolute adverb; neither can be qualified:

> He asserts that Britain, not quite uniquely, is in the grip of a New Labour political class that has little understanding of the meaning of truth and scant regard for it anyway. (book review)

Also, what is the point of 'not quite uniquely' here? Surely only one country, Britain, is run by New Labour.

'Verbal', which can mean either related to words (verbal reasoning) or spoken (verbal agreement), can be confusing:

> What strikes me most is the inarticulacy of LeRoy's speech . . . And while there is no reason for authors to be verbally articulate, I cannot find the pulse here. (feature)

10

Foreign words

There are many foreign words and phrases in current English. As the world's most flexible and widely used language, English constantly adopts new words from elsewhere. In particular, the flow of words from French has not stopped since the Norman invasion.

There are also many words and phrases taken from Greek and Latin still used by some people. As the classics continue to lose ground in schools, fewer and fewer readers are familiar with this vocabulary, so there is a strong case for finding English equivalents.

Use words of foreign origin accurately but not pretentiously, always asking yourself: 'Will my reader understand this?' To put it another way, do not litter your copy with words that would need to be italicised because they are unfamiliar. In general, if a word needs italics, translate it into English.

But if you do use foreign words to spice up your copy, be accurate.

- Do not follow the *Daily Mail* subeditor who headlined a story about a French mayor trying to resist the English invasion of his town:

    ALLEZ LES ANGLAIS!

    Instead of what was meant ('English, go away', which would have been 'Allez-vous-en'), this says the opposite: 'Go on.'

- The French word *embonpoint* is not in fact a euphemism for an ample bosom but an everyday word for portliness à la Hercule Poirot. Which makes utter nonsense of this clever-sounding sentence in a *Guardian* sports report:

    The current version of Buster Mathis boasts not just a Michelinman waist but an *embonpoint* that would give him a better shot at starring in the next Wonderbra poster than winning a boxing title.

- The *Spectator* columnist Taki accidentally labelled himself an anti-Semite by misusing the term *soi-disant* – he thought it meant 'so-called' when in fact it translates as 'self-styled'.

- When the Tory politician Alan Clark used the phrase 'economical with the actualité' (as a variant on the original 'economical with the truth') he was making a pretentious blunder: *actualité* means 'topicality' or 'current events'. But this has not stopped the phrase being repeated: it sounds impressive.

Be careful with translated words.

- *Time* magazine mistranslated an interview with Gérard Depardieu confusing the primary meaning in French of *assister à* (to be present at) with its English echo (to help in). As a result the unfortunate French actor (who had grown up in a rough neighbourhood and, as a boy, had *witnessed* a rape) found himself widely accused of being a rapist.

- When interior minister Nicolas Sarkozy promised in October 2005 to rid France's estates of '*la racaille*' (rabble), the stronger word 'scum' was used instead by the British and American press.

English and French have many *faux amis* – two words from different languages that sound similar but have different meanings. So never guess the meaning of a French word.

Try not to mix the foreign and the English. Say either 'a year' or 'per annum' not 'per year'. (But 'miles per hour/mph' and 'miles per gallon/ mpg' are sanctioned by usage.)

If your house style includes accents, make sure that you use them consistently. For example, 'paté' and 'emigré' are howlers: they should be *pâté* and *émigré*. And watch your spelling of foreign words: *de rigueur* includes the letter 'u' twice; *restaurateur* has no 'n'; *bête noire* has an 'e' at the end. (For the plurals of foreign words see Chapter 5, **Spelling**, p. 56.)

Also note that French words change their spelling in the feminine and the plural: the adjective bas (low) becomes basse when used with a feminine noun; most nouns and adjectives take 's' in the plural.

Below is a selection of foreign words and phrases in current English, followed by some examples of common classical references. Use both lists with care – when in doubt, always translate into English.

ab initio: from the beginning (Latin)

actualité: topicality or current events, *not* truth (French)

AD/anno domini: in the year of the Lord (Latin)

addendum/a: something to be added, eg to a book (Latin)

ad hoc: for this special purpose (Latin), so also adhocery, adhocism, the use of ad hoc measures

ad hominem: personal, used of an argument that attacks the character of an opponent rather than their argument (Latin: 'to the man')

ad infinitum: endlessly (Latin)

ad lib(itum): without restraint, impromptu (Latin: 'according to pleasure')

ad nauseam: to a sickening extent (Latin)

aegis: protection (Greek)

affidavit: written declaration on oath (Latin)

aficionado: fan, originally of bullfighting (Spanish)

à fond: thoroughly, in depth (French)

a fortiori: with stronger reason (Latin)

agent provocateur: person who leads others into committing unlawful acts (French)

agitprop: political propaganda (Russian)

aide-mémoire: reminder, written summary (French)

à la: in the style of – a short form of 'à la mode de': 'à la Hercule Poirot'

à la carte: with the freedom to pick and choose (French)

à la mode: fashionable (French)
       (French cookery) of beef – stewed in wine
       (American cookery) served with icecream

à la mode de: in the style of (French)

alfresco: in the open air (Italian)

alibi: evidence that the accused was elsewhere when a crime was being committed (Latin)

alma mater: particular school or university to its students (Latin: 'bounteous mother')

alpha and omega: beginning and end (Greek alphabet)

am/ante meridiem: in the morning (Latin)

amanuensis: literary assistant, especially one who writes to dictation or copies from manuscripts (Latin)

amen: so be it, agreed (Hebrew)

amour propre: self-esteem, vanity (French)

anathema: deeply offensive (Greek)

ancien régime: the old system (French: that before the 1789 revolution)

angst: anxiety of a general kind (German)

annus mirabilis: wonderful year (Latin)

Anschluss: take-over, eg of Austria by Nazi Germany in 1938 (German: 'union')

ante: fixed stake in poker (Latin: 'before'), hence up/raise the ante – increase costs, demands, etc

ante-bellum: before the war (Latin), particularly used of the American civil war

antipasto: first course (Italian: 'before food')

aperçu: insight (French: 'noticed')

apéritif: drink before a meal (French)

apogee: highest point (Greek)

à point: just right (French)

a posteriori: (of reasoning) from effect to cause (Latin)

apparatchik: member of party machine, originally apparat of Communist Party (Russian)

après-ski: fun and games after skiing (French)

a priori: (of reasoning) from cause to effect (Latin)

apropos (of): to the point (French), also used in the opposite sense to mean 'incidentally'

arriviste: ambitious, self-seeking person (French)

à trois: see *ménage*

au contraire: on the contrary (French)

au courant: well-informed, up-to-date (French)

au fait (with): well informed, expert (in) (French)

au fond: fundamentally (French)

au naturel: cooked plainly or served without dressing (French)

au pair: foreign girl who does light domestic work in exchange for room and board (French: 'on equal terms')

au secours: help! (French)

autres temps, autres moeurs: customs change with the times (French)

avant-garde: trend-setting artists, writers, etc (French)

avant la lettre: before the definition was invented (French)

ave: hail (Latin)

bain-marie: pot of boiling water in which another pot is placed to cook slowly (French)

bête noire: bugbear (French)

bien pensant: right-thinking

billet-doux: love letter (French)

bint: derogatory word for girl (Arabic: 'daughter')

blasé: indifferent to pleasure through familiarity (French)

blitz: sudden strong attack (German: 'lightning'), hence the blitzkrieg attack on Poland in 1939

blond(e): fair-haired (French) – see also Agreement, p. 60

bona fide: genuine (Latin: 'in good faith'), hence bona fides: genuineness, proof of trustworthiness – *note* bona fides is singular

bonhomie: genial manner (French)

bon mot: witty saying (French)

bonne-bouche: tasty morsel (French)

bon vivant: person who enjoys life, particularly good food (French), not 'bon viveur'

boudoir: woman's small private room (French)

bra/brassière: women's undergarment to support the breasts (French) *but* in modern French une brassière is a baby's vest – a bra is 'un soutien-gorge'

branché: switched on, trendy (French)

bric-à-brac: odd items of furniture, ornaments, etc (French)

brunet(te): dark-haired (French) – see also Agreement p. 60

ca/circa: about (Latin)

canard: false report, hoax (French)

carpe diem: enjoy the present moment (Latin: 'seize the day')

carte blanche: freedom to do as one thinks (French: 'blank page')

casus belli: act or situation seen to justify war (Latin)

caveat: warning (Latin)

caveat emptor: let the buyer beware (Latin)

(un) certain age: no longer young (French)

ceteris paribus: other things being equal (Latin)

cf/confer: compare (Latin)

(à) chacun son goût: everyone to their own taste (French), not 'chacun à son goût'

chaperon(e): older person supervising girl or unmarried woman (French) – see also Agreement, p. 60

chargé d'affaires: senior diplomat, eg ambassador's deputy (French)

château: French castle, large country house or wine property

châtelaine: mistress of château (French)

chef d'oeuvre: masterpiece (French)

chutzpah: effrontery, impudence (Yiddish)

cliché: hackneyed phrase or idea (French: 'printing plate')

cogito ergo sum: I think, therefore I am – starting point in philosophy of Descartes (Latin)

comme il faut: proper (French)

compos mentis: sane (Latin)

confidant(e): person to confide in (French) – see also Agreement p. 60

cons: see *pros and cons*

contra: against (Latin)

contretemps: hitch, quarrel (French)

coquette: flirt (French)

cordon bleu: (cook) of the highest excellence (French: 'blue ribbon')

cordon sanitaire: isolating barrier (French)

corpus delicti: evidence of a crime, eg corpse (Latin)

corrigenda: corrections (Latin)

cortège: funeral procession (French)

cosi fan tutte: what all women do (Italian)

couchette: railway sleeping berth that is convertible by day into ordinary seat (French)

coup d'état: sudden overthrow of government especially by force (French)

coup de foudre: love at first sight (French: 'thunderbolt')

coup de grâce: death blow (French: 'mercy blow')

coup de main: surprise attack (French) *but* in modern French 'un coup de main' is a helping hand

(la) crème de la crème: the elite (French)

cri de coeur: cry from the heart (French)

crime passionel: crime, eg murder, caused by sexual passion (French)

crise de conscience: crisis of conscience (French)

cui bono?: who stands to gain? (Latin)

cul-de-sac: dead end, blind alley (French: 'bottom of the sack') *but* in modern French 'voie sans issu' or 'impasse' is far more common – 'cul' is seen as coarse

culottes: divided skirt (French) *but* in modern French 'une culotte' (singular) is a pair of panties/underpants

curettage: surgical scraping to remove tissue or growth (French)

cv/curriculum vitae: biographical summary (Latin)

danse macabre: dance of death (French)

débâcle: sudden disastrous collapse (French)

débutant(e): beginner (French) – see also Agreement, p. 60

déclassé: reduced in social standing (French)

décolletage: a low neckline (French)

décolleté: low cut, wearing a low-cut dress (French)

de facto: in fact, actual (Latin)

dégagé: free from constraint, politically uncommitted (French)

De Glanville: like most French surnames starting with 'de', when anglicised it begins 'De'

de haut en bas: condescending (French)

déjà vu: feeling that something similar has been experienced before (French)

de jure: by right (Latin)

de mortuis nil nisi bonum: say nothing but good of the dead (Latin)

dénouement: resolution of plot (French)

Deo volente: God willing (Latin)

de rigueur: strictly necessary (French)

derrière: euphemism for buttocks (French)

déshabillé: partly dressed, not undressed (French)

détente: easing of tension between countries (French)

de trop: not wanted, in the way (French: 'excessive')

deus ex machina: contrived solution of plot difficulty in fiction (Latin: 'god from the machinery')

dictum: saying (Latin)

digestif: strongly alcoholic drink after a meal (French)

dishabille: anglicised version of déshabillé – see above

divorcé(e): divorced person (French) – but prefer the anglicised 'divorcee' for both men and women

do/ditto: the same thing (Italian)

dolce far niente: sweet idleness (Italian)

(la) dolce vita: life of luxury (Italian: 'sweet life')

doppelgänger: ghostly double (German: 'double goer')

double entente: word or phrase with two meanings, one usually indecent (French), not 'double entendre'

dreich: dreary (Scottish)

droit du seigneur/jus primae noctis: feudal lord's alleged right to have sex with a vassal's bride on the wedding night (French/Latin)

dulce et decorum est pro patria mori: it is sweet and glorious to die for one's country – Horace (Latin)

dum spiro, spero: while I breathe, I hope (Latin)

éclat: ostentatious brilliance (French)

effluvium: offensive smell (Latin)

eg/exempli gratia: for example (Latin: 'by way of example')

élan: zest and vigour (French)

embarrass de richesses: over-abundance of pleasures or resources (French)

embonpoint: stoutness, portliness (French: 'in good form') not 'ample bosom'

éminence grise: power behind the throne (French: 'grey eminence')

en bloc: all at the same time (French)

en masse: all together (French)

entente cordiale: friendly understanding, eg between Britain and France in 1904 (French)

entrée: first course all over the world except in north America where it is the main course; also entry in other contexts (French)

ergo: therefore (Latin)

erratum/a: error(s) in writing or printing (Latin)

ersatz: substitute, fake (German)

et al/alii, aliae, alia: and others (Latin)

etc/et cetera: and the rest, and so on (Latin)

ex cathedra: with authority (Latin: 'from the chair of office')
ex gratia: as a favour, not from obligation (Latin)
ex officio: because of a person's official position (Latin)
ex parte: from one side only (Latin)
ex post facto: retrospective (Latin)

factotum: servant who does all kinds of work (Latin)
fait accompli: a thing already done, and so irreversible (French)
fakir: religious beggar or ascetic in India (Arabic)
fatwa(h): Muslim sentence of death (Arabic)
faute de mieux: for want of anything better (French)
faux amis: two similar words from different languages that have different
     meanings – eg the French 'veste' is not a vest but a jacket (French:
     'false friends')
faux pas: embarrassing blunder (French: 'false step')
felo de se: suicide (Anglo-Latin: 'felon of himself')
femme fatale: dangerous and irresistibly attractive woman (French)
festina lente: more haste, less speed (Latin)
festschrift: celebratory publication (German)
fid def/fidei defensor: defender of the faith (Latin)
floreat: may it flourish (Latin)
folie de grandeur: delusions of importance (French)
frisson: shiver, thrill (French)
furore: uproar (Latin)

Gastarbeiter: migrant worker (German: 'guest worker')
gaucho: South American cowboy; hence 'gauchos', women's knee-length
     trousers (Spanish)
gaudeamus: let us rejoice (Latin)
gemütlich: cosy (German)
gestalt: organised whole or unit (German)
Gesundheit: good health – to a person who has sneezed (German)
glasnost: Soviet policy of openness launched by Mikhail Gorbachev
     (Russian)
Götterdämmerung: twilight of the gods (German)
goy: Gentile (Hebrew)
grand guignol: horror drama – from Grand Guignol, a Paris theatre
     specialising in horror
gringo: Spanish-American for English speaker
gulag: labour camp for political prisoners – from Solzhenitsyn's book *The
     Gulag Archipelago* (Russian)

habeas corpus: writ requiring that a person be brought before a judge or
     into court (Latin: 'have the body')

habitué: inhabitant or frequent visitor (French)
hara-kiri: ritual suicide (Japanese)
hoi polloi: derogatory term for the masses (Greek); since 'hoi' means 'the', 'the' in front of 'hoi' is redundant
honoris causa: as a mark of esteem (Latin)
hors de combat: out of action (French: 'out of the fight')
hors d'oeuvre: first course (French: 'outside the work')

ibid(em): in the same place (Latin)
idée fixe: obsession (French)
ie/id est: that is to say (Latin)
imbroglio: tangled situation (Italian)
impasse: deadlock (French) – see also *cul-de-sac*
imprimatur: licence to print a book (Latin: 'let it be printed')
in absentia: in one's absence (Latin)
inamorata(o): the beloved (Latin)
in camera: in secret, in a judge's private chambers (Latin: 'in the chamber')
incognito: unknown, in disguise (Italian)
in extremis: at the point of death, in very great difficulties (Latin)
in flagrante delicto: caught in the act (Latin: 'while the crime is burning')
infra dig/dignitatem: beneath one's dignity (Latin)
ingénue: innocent, naive young woman, especially on the stage (French: 'ingenuous')
in loco parentis: in place of a parent (Latin)
in memoriam: in memory of (Latin)
in petto: in secret (Italian)
in situ: in its present or original place (Latin)
inter alia: among other things (Latin)
interim: the meantime, provisional (Latin)
interregnum: period between two reigns (Latin)
Intifada: Palestinian uprising (1987) and continued resistance to Israeli occupation (Arabic)
in toto: entirely (Latin)
in utero: in the womb (Latin)
in vino veritas: truth is told under the influence of alcohol (Latin: 'in wine is truth')
in vitro: in the test tube (Latin)
in vivo: in the living organism (Latin)
iota: very small amount (smallest letter in Greek alphabet)
ipse dixit: dogmatic statement (Latin: 'he himself said it')
ipso facto: by that very fact (Latin)

jawohl: yes, indeed (German)

jeunesse dorée: fashionable, rich young people (French)
jeu d'esprit: witticism (French)
jus primae noctis: see *droit du seigneur*

kamikaze: suicide attack, originally by Japanese airforce
      (Japanese: 'divine wind')

laissez/laisser-faire: policy of non-interference (French)
laudator temporis acti: person living in the past (Latin: 'praiser of past
      times')
Lebensraum: living space, Nazi justification for German expansion (German)
leitmotiv/f: recurring theme (German)
lèse-majesté: treason, affront to dignity (French)
liaison: relationship (eg sexual, military) not individual encounter
      (French)
lingua franca: common language used by the people of an area where
      several languages are spoken (Italian: 'Frankish language')
loc cit/loco citato: in the place just quoted (Latin)
locum (tenens): deputy, substitute (Latin)
locus classicus: best-known or most authoritative example (Latin)

macho: aggressively male, hence machismo, the cult of this (Spanish)
magnum opus: great work (Latin)
mañana: tomorrow, in the indefinite future (Spanish)
mandamus: writ from higher court (Latin: 'we command')
manqué: having failed, as in 'poet manqué' (French)
maquis: French guerrilla resistance movement
mea culpa: through my own fault (Latin)
mélange: mixture (French)
memento mori: reminder of death (Latin)
ménage à trois: household of three people, each one having
      a sexual relationship with at least one of the others
      (French)
mens rea: criminal intent (Latin)
mens sana in corpore sano: a healthy mind in a healthy body
      (Latin)
mésalliance: marriage with a social inferior (French)
métier: trade (French)
métissage: interbreeding (French)
mirabile dictu: wonderful to relate (Latin)
mo/modus operandi: way of working, eg by criminal (Latin)
modus vivendi: arrangement, compromise (Latin: 'way of living')
monstre sacré: powerful and eccentric public figure (French)

mot juste: exact word (French)
mutatis mutandis: with necessary changes (Latin)

nb/nota bene: take notice (Latin)
né(e): originally named (French: 'born')
négligé: woman's loose, flimsy dressing gown (French)
nem con/nemine contradicente: without opposition (Latin)
ne plus ultra: the ultimate (Latin)
nihil obstat: permission to print (Latin: 'nothing hinders')
nil desperandum: never despair – Horace (Latin)
nirvana: blissful state (Sanskrit)
nisi: to take effect unless (Latin)
noblesse oblige: rank imposes obligations (French)
noli me tangere: don't touch me (Latin)
nolle prosequi: suspension of legal action (Latin)
nom de plume: pen name, pseudonym (French) *but* the modern French
       phrase is 'nom de guerre'
non compos mentis: not of sound mind (Latin)
non sequitur: conclusion that does not follow from premise(s),
       disconnected remark (Latin)
nostrum: favourite remedy (Latin: 'our own')
nouveau riche: person with newly acquired wealth but lacking in refinement
       (French)

obiter dictum/a: cursory remark(s) (Latin)
objet d'art: small article with artistic value (French)
omerta: the Mafia code of honour compelling silence (Italian dialect)
omnibus: widely comprehensive, origin of 'bus' – large public road vehicle
       (Latin)
on dit: item of gossip, hearsay (French)
op cit/opere citato: in the same book as was mentioned before (Latin)
outré: excessive, eccentric (French), *but* in French it means 'scandalised'

pa/per annum: a year (Latin)
pace: with due deference – used in disagreeing with somebody (Latin)
paean: hymn of praise (Latin)
papabile: (of a prospective pope) electable (Italian)
paparazzo/i: snatch photographer(s) of famous people (Italian)
par excellence: more than all others (French)
pari passu: at an equal rate of progress, simultaneously and equally (Latin)
parti pris: bias, prejudice (French)
passé: past its sell-by date (French)
passim: throughout (Latin)
pax vobiscum: peace be with you (Latin)

peccavi: I have sinned (Latin)
per ardua ad astra: through a steep climb to the stars (Latin)
per capita: a head (Latin)
per cent: for each hundred (Latin)
per contra: by contrast (Latin)
per diem: a day (Latin)
per se: in itself (Latin)
perestroika: restructuring of political and economic system in the Soviet
    Union of the 1980s
persona (non) grata: acceptable (or not), especially to foreign government
    (Latin)
petitio principii: begging the question (Latin) – see p. 112
pièce de résistance: the showpiece, especially in a meal
    (French)
pied-à-terre: second home, usually in city or town (French)
pis aller: makeshift (French)
placet: permission is given (Latin)
pm/post meridiem: afternoon (Latin)
poste restante: post office department where mail is kept until collected
    (French)
post hoc ergo propter hoc: fallacious argument that A causes B because it is
    followed by B (Latin)
post-partum: after childbirth (Latin)
pourboire: tip (French)
pour encourager les autres: as an example to others (French)
pp/per pro/per procurationem: by proxy, on behalf of (Latin)
précis: summary (French)
prima facie: at first sight (Latin)
primus inter pares: first among equals (Latin)
pro bono (publico): for the public good, particularly used of lawyers working
    as unpaid volunteers (Latin)
pro-forma: (of an account) official form for completion (Latin)
pro patria: for one's country (Latin)
pro rata: in proportion (Latin)
pros and cons: arguments for and against (Latin)
protégé(e): person under someone's patronage (French)
pro tem(pore): for the time being (Latin)

qed/quod erat demonstrandum: which was to be demonstrated, proved
    (Latin)
qua: in the capacity of (Latin)
quid pro quo: something given, taken, offered for something else (Latin)
(on the) qui vive: on the alert (French sentry's challenge: 'long live who?')

quondam: former (Latin)
quorum: fixed number of members necessary for a valid meeting (Latin)
qv/quod vide: which see (Latin)

raison d'être: reason for existence (French)
realpolitik: practical politics (German)
réchauffé: reheated, rehashed (French)
recherché: rare or exotic (French)
recto: front or right-hand page of book (Latin)
reductio ad absurdum: demonstrating the falsity of a proposition by showing
    that its logical extension is absurd (Latin)
repêchage: extra heat in sporting event giving those eliminated a second
    chance to go on to the final (French: 'fishing out again')
requiem: Catholic mass, dirge for the dead (Latin)
rigor mortis: stiffening of the body after death (Latin)
RIP/requiescat in pace: may he/she rest in peace (Latin)
rite de passage: ceremony marking a new stage in a person's life (French)
roué: dissolute (old) man (French: 'broken on the wheel')

samizdat: underground literature, originally in Soviet Union (Russian)
sans: without (French)
savoir-faire: knowhow (French)
savoir-vivre: knowing how to live (French)
Schadenfreude: malicious delight in another's misfortune (German)
sd/sine die: indefinitely (Latin)
semper fidelis: always faithful (Latin)
seq(uens): following (Latin)
seriatim: in succession (Latin)
shmatte: rag, shabby garment (Yiddish)
sic: written here as in the original – used to mark mistakes in quotations
    (Latin: 'so, thus')
sine qua non: essential condition (Latin)
smörgåsbord: buffet meal of various dishes (Swedish)
soi-disant: self-styled, not so-called (French)
soigné(e): well-groomed (French)
sotto voce: in an undertone or aside (Italian)
status quo (ante): existing state of things (before change) (Latin)
stet: cancel correction (Latin: 'let it stand')
stumm/shtoom: silent (Yiddish from German)
Sturm und Drang: highly emotional eighteenth-century German literary
    movement (storm and stress)
succès d'estime: critical, as opposed to popular, success (French)
sub judice: under judicial consideration, so not able to be discussed (Latin)

subpoena: writ commanding attendance (Latin: 'under penalty')
sub rosa: in secrecy, in confidence (Latin: 'under the rose', a symbol of secrecy)
sui generis: the only one of its kind (Latin)
supra: above (Latin)

table d'hôte: fixed price meal (French)
tabula rasa: clean slate (Latin: 'scraped tablet')
Te Deum: hymn of praise and thanksgiving (Latin)
terra firma: dry land or the ground, as opposed to water or sky, originally the mainland as opposed to islands (Latin: 'solid earth')
terra incognita: unknown or unexplored region (Latin)
tête-à-tête: one-to-one, in private (French)
tour d'horizon: broad general survey (French)
trahison des clercs: betrayal of standards by intellectuals (French)
tricoteuse: French Revolutionary woman who knitted beneath the guillotine (French: 'knitter')
troika: team of three (Russian)
touché: hit acknowledged, in argument as in fencing (French)
tour de force: outstanding performance (French)

Übermensch: superman (German)
ubi supra: where mentioned above (Latin)
uhuru: freedom, national independence (Swahili)
ujamaa: kibbutz-type village community in Tanzania (Swahili)
ult(imo): in the last month (Latin)
ultra vires: beyond one's powers (Latin)

v/vide infra/supra: see (below/above) (Latin)
v/vs/versus: against (Latin)
vade-mecum: pocket reference book (Latin: 'go with me')
vale: farewell (Latin)
verbatim: word for word (Latin)
verboten: forbidden (German)
verb sap/verbum sapienti sat est: no further explanation needed (Latin: 'a word is enough for the wise')
verkramp: narrow-minded, illiberal in apartheid South Africa (Afrikaans)
verlig: enlightened, liberal in apartheid South Africa (Afrikaans)
vice anglais: corporal punishment for sexual gratification, sodomy (French: 'English vice')
victor ludorum: school champion on sports day (Latin)
vieux jeu: old hat (French: 'old game')
virgo intacta: virgin (Latin)
vis-à-vis: in relation to (French: 'face-to-face')

viva (voce): oral exam (Latin)
vivat: long live (Latin)
viz/videlicet: namely (Latin)
vo/verso: back or left-hand page of book (Latin)
volenti non fit injuria: no injury is done to a consenting party (Latin)
volte-face: complete change of attitude (French)
voortrekker: Boer pioneer in South Africa (Afrikaans)
voulu: contrived in English (but not in French)
vox pop(uli): public opinion, street interview (Latin: 'voice of the people')

wagon-lit: sleeping car (French)
wunderkind: child prodigy (German)

zeitgeist: spirit of the age (German)

Common classical references

All the examples below might be found in an upmarket newspaper such as the *Observer* or a weekly review such as the *Spectator*. Some, such as 'aphrodisiac', 'cynic', 'erotic' and 'platonic', are everyday expressions. The problem, as always, is in deciding which ones your reader will recognise and not stumble over.

Whereas most are traditional, one or two have recently acquired new meanings. As sport has become increasingly dominated by money – 'professional' in its worst sense – 'corinthian' is more and more a word of praise for the true amateur. 'Trojan horse' now suggests a covert computer virus as well as a political fifth columnist.

achilles heel: a person's weakness – the Greek demi-god Achilles was invulnerable except in the heel
acropolis: citadel, especially that of Athens
Adonis: handsome youth – Aphrodite loved him
Aeneid: Latin epic poem by Virgil; its hero is Aeneas
Amazon: strong, tall, warlike woman – in Greek mythology the Amazons cut off their right breasts to improve their archery
ambrosia: the food and drink of the Greek gods – it gave them everlasting youth and beauty
aphrodisiac: something that arouses sexual desire – from Aphrodite
Aphrodite: beautiful woman, the Greek goddess of love
Apollo: handsome youth, the Greek sun god; hence 'Apollonian', serene, rational (opposite of Dionysian)

Arcadia: mountainous district in Greece where people lived a simple rural life with much music and dancing

Argonaut: adventurer – from the Greeks who sailed with Jason in the Argos in search of the golden fleece

Athene (also Athena): Greek goddess of wisdom; hence Athens, the city, and Athenaeum, a temple of Athene, so a place of learning

Atlas: strong man – the Titan who held up the pillars of the universe

Augean stables: something rotten or corrupt, somewhere in need of a good clean – Hercules did the trick by diverting the river Alpheus through the stables

Augustan age (of literature): classical, refined – taken from that of the Roman emperor Augustus Caesar and applied to eighteenth-century England

Bacchus: Roman god of wine – hence bacchanals, drunken revels, etc

Cadmus: see *dragon's teeth*

Caesar: autocrat – from the first Roman emperor, Julius Caesar

caesarian section: delivery of a child by cutting through the abdomen – Julius Caesar was said to have been born this way

Caesar's wife: someone who must be above suspicion

Cassandra: daughter of Priam, King of Troy; she had the gift of prophecy but not the knack of making people believe her; hence 'a prophet of doom who is not heeded' (and a celebrated *Daily Mirror* columnist)

centaur: mythical creature, half-man half-horse

Cerberus: the monster that guarded the entrance to Hades

Charybdis: see *Scylla*

chimerical: imaginary, fanciful – from the chimera, a fire-breathing monster with a lion's head, a goat's body and a serpent's tail

Circe: beautiful sorcerer; hence Circean

corinthian: from Corinth in Greece – in architecture and literary style over-elaborate but in sport showing the spirit of the true amateur: playing the game for its own sake

cornucopia: horn of plenty – a goat's horn overflowing with flowers, fruit and corn

Croesus: King of Lydia and fabulously rich

cross the Rubicon: see *Rubicon*

Cupid: Roman god of love, depicted as a naked boy with wings, bow and arrow; hence Cupid's bow, the upper lip shaped like an archery double bow, and Cupid's dart, the power of love

Cyclops: giant with one eye in the middle of his forehead

cynic: a public pessimist about human motives – from the Cynics, a sect of philosophers founded by Antisthenes of Athens

Daedelus: the Greek artist who constructed the Cretan labyrinth and made
wings for his son Icarus and himself

Damocles: was taught the insecurity of happiness by sitting through
a feast with a sword hanging over his head – from a single
hair

Delphic: difficult to interpret like the oracle of Delphi

Diogenic: cynical, like the Cynic philosopher Diogenes

Dionysian: sensual, abandoned – from Dionysus, the Greek god of wine
(opposite of Apollonian)

draconian: extremely severe like the laws of Draco of Athens

dragon's teeth: the teeth of the dragon killed by Cadmus, the founder of
Thebes; he sowed them and they turned into armed men who fought
among themselves until only five were left

Elysian fields (champs élysées): any delightful place – from Elysium, the
home of the blessed after death

Epicurean: person devoted to sensual enjoyment – from Epicurus, the Greek
philosopher

Eros: Greek god of love; hence erotic, etc

Fabian tactics: delaying, cautious – from the Roman general Fabius
Cunctator, who saved Rome by wearing down the Carthaginian general
Hannibal; hence 'the Fabian Society', formed to encourage the gradual
spread of socialist ideas

golden fleece: see *Argonaut*

Gordian knot: intricate knot tied by Gordius, King of Phrygia, and cut by
Alexander the Great

Gorgon: one of three female monsters; hence 'an ugly or formidable woman'

Greek gifts: given with intent to harm

Greek god: beautiful man

Hades: the Greek underworld, roamed by the souls of the dead

halcyon days: a time of peace and happiness – from halcyon, the kingfisher,
once supposed to make a floating nest on the sea, thus calming it

harpy: rapacious monster, part-woman part-bird; hence a greedy,
cruel woman

Heracles: Greek form of Hercules

Hercules: hero of superhuman strength who had to complete the 12 labours;
hence herculean, etc

Hermes: Greek god of herdsmen, arts, theft and eloquence, the messenger
of the gods; also identified with the Egyptian god Thoth, founder of
alchemy, astrology, etc

hermetic: completely sealed – from Hermes, the Greek name for Thoth

Hippocratic oath: doctor's promise to follow medical code of ethics, first drawn up by the Greek physician Hippocrates

Homeric: refers to Homer, the Greek epic poet said to have written the Iliad and the Odyssey

hubris: arrogance such as to invite disaster – from Greek tragedy

Icarus: rashly ambitious person – Icarus, son of Daedalus, flew so high that the sun melted the wax with which his wings were fastened and he fell to his death

Iliad: Greek epic poem, ascribed to Homer, describing the climax of the siege of Troy

Janus: Roman two-faced god

Jason: see *Argonaut*

Jove: another name for Jupiter; hence the archaic 'by Jove'

junoesque: large, buxom and beautiful – from Juno, the wife of Jupiter

Jupiter: chief Roman god; the largest planet

labyrinth: maze – the Cretan labyrinth was constructed by Daedalus to contain the Minotaur, a bull-headed monster

laconic: terse – from Laconia, whose capital was Sparta

Lethe: river of the underworld causing oblivion to those who drank from it

lotus-eater: indolent lover of luxury, one of a people described by Homer as eating the fruit of the lotus and living in a state of dreamy forgetfulness

Lucullan: (of a banquet) in the lavish style of the Roman Lucullus

Marathon: scene of a Greek victory over the Persians, from where a messenger ran to Athens to report the good news; thus a long-distance race or other test of endurance

Mars: Roman god of war; the planet next after earth in terms of distance from the sun

Medusa: best known of the three Gorgons, whose head, with snakes for hair, turned observers to stone; hence medusa, the jellyfish

Mercury: Roman god of merchandise, theft and eloquence, the messenger of the gods, and the planet nearest the sun; hence mercurial, lively, volatile (also related to the metal mercury)

Midas: King of Phrygia whose touch turned everything to gold

Mount Olympus: see *Olympus*

Muse: one of the nine daughters of Zeus; thus poetic inspiration

Myrmidon: one of a tribe of warriors who accompanied Achilles to Troy

narcissism: self-obsession – from the Greek youth Narkissos who pined away for love of his own image

nectar: the drink of the gods

Nemesis: the Greek goddess of retribution

Neptune: the Roman sea god and a remote planet of the solar system

nymph: semi-divine spirit inhabiting woods, rivers, etc; beautiful young woman; hence 'nymphet', a sexually attractive and precocious girl, and 'nymphomania' (of women), insatiable sexual desire

Odyssey: Greek epic poem, ascribed to Homer, describing the wanderings of Odysseus (Ulysses) after the Trojan War; so any long wandering

Oedipus: king of Thebes who unwittingly killed his father and married his mother; hence 'Oedipus complex', describing a son's hostility to his father and intense love of his mother

Olympia: place where the original Olympic games were held

Olympiad: originally the period of four years between Olympic games; now a celebration of the modern games or other international contest

Olympian: godlike person; competitor in games

Olympic games (Olympics): international athletic and other contests held every four years since 1896, a revival of the original Greek games

Olympus: mountain where the Greek gods lived, heaven

Orphean: melodious – from the musician Orpheus whose lyre playing could move inanimate objects

Pan: Greek god of pastures, flocks and woods, worshipped in Arcadia, fond of music

Pandora: the first woman, who opened a box she was given, releasing all the ills of human life

Pantheon: temple of all the gods; complete mythology

Parnassus: Greek mountain sacred to Apollo and the Muses

Parthenon: temple of Athene on the Acropolis in Athens

Parthian shot: arrow fired on the turn by Parthian warrior; hence 'parting shot'

Pegasus: winged horse that sprang from Medusa's blood; hence 'a flight of inspiration or genius'

Periclean: of the Athenian golden age of Pericles

Phaedra complex: difficult relationship between step-parent and son/daughter – from Phaedra who killed herself after being rejected by her stepson

Philippics: three orations by Demosthenes of Athens against Philip of Macedon

platonic: refers to the philosophy of Plato, particularly the idea of love between souls without sexual feeling

Poseidon: the Greek sea god

Priapus: Greek and Roman god of procreation; hence priapic (of men), obsessed with sexuality

Prometheus: he stole fire from heaven so Zeus chained him to a rock

protean: assuming different shapes and sizes – from the Greek sea god Proteus

pyrrhic victory: one achieved at too great a cost as by Pyrrhus, King of Epirus, over the Romans

Rubicon: a stream that marked the boundary between Julius Caesar's province of Cisalpine Gaul and Italy – when he crossed it he effectively declared war on Rome; hence 'to cross the Rubicon' is to take a decisive, irrevocable step

Sapphic: refers to the Greek woman poet Sappho of Lesbos who was said to be homosexual

Saturn: Roman god of agriculture, whose festival in December, the Saturnalia, was the occasion for unrestrained merrymaking; and the planet that was believed to induce a melancholy temperament – hence saturnine, gloomy

satyr: Greek god of the woodlands with tail and long ears, depicted by the Romans as part-goat; a lecherous man

Scylla and Charybdis: two monsters that occupied the two sides of the Straits of Messina between Italy and Sicily; hence 'between Scylla and Charybdis' means a perilous route in which avoiding one danger brings the traveller closer to the other

siren: fascinating woman, bewitching singer – from the sirens, sea nymphs whose seductive songs lured sailors to their deaths; hence 'a warning signal'

Sisyphean: refers to Sisyphus, King of Corinth, who was condemned to roll a stone up a hill – as it neared the top it would roll down again; hence a laborious and futile task

Socratic: refers to the philosophy and teaching method of the philosopher Socrates – based on asking a series of simple questions

sophistry: specious or fallacious reasoning – from the sophists who taught in Greece

sop to Cerberus: the drugged food given to Cerberus to enable Aeneas to enter Hades; hence something to appease, a bribe

Spartacist: follower of Spartacus who led a slave revolt against Rome; hence extreme German communist in 1918 revolution

spartan: tough, austere, militaristic – from the Greek city of Sparta

sphinx: monster in Greek mythology with the head of a woman and the body of a lion which asked travellers riddles – then strangled those that could not solve them; also Egyptian stone figure, particularly the huge enigmatic-looking one near the pyramids at Giza; hence 'a mysterious person or thing'

stentorian: loud, powerful (voice) – from Stentor, a Greek herald in the Iliad

stoic(al): indifferent to pleasure or pain – from the Stoics of Athens

Stygian: black, gloomy – from the Styx, one of the rivers of Hades

sword of Damocles: see *Damocles*

Sybarite: lover of luxury – from Sybaris, a Greek city in ancient Italy

Thebes: name of the capital of both ancient Boeotia in Greece and Upper Egypt

thespian: jocular word for actor – from Thespis, the founder of Greek tragedy

Titan: one of a family of giants, the offspring of Uranus (heaven) and Gaea (earth); hence a person of great strength; also the sun god

triumvirate: rule by three men – originally of Rome by Pompey, Crassus and Caesar

Trojan: solid, dependable, courageous person – from the citizens of Troy

Trojan horse: huge wooden horse in which the Greeks hid to enter the city of Troy; hence fifth columnist and computer program that by subterfuge breaches the security of a system in order to damage it

Ulysses: Latin name for Greek hero Odysseus

Venus: Roman goddess of love and the most brilliant planet

vestal: refers to Roman goddess Vesta; vestal virgins kept the sacred fire burning on her altar

wooden horse: see *Trojan horse*

Zeus: the greatest of the Greek gods

zephyr: west wind, especially as personified as a god; soft, gentle breeze

Mistakes

We can't supply our troops in Iraq with working radios or a legal causus belli. (column)

'Causus' should be 'casus'.

Anyone who denies that the British class system is the most complex and unfathomable in the world will need to establish from John why a fibbing Fettes alumni has produced such a diametrically opposite reaction in him. (column)

'Alumni' (plural) should be 'alumnus' (singular)

> This was the 1960s, remember, and rebels with or without a cause
> were de jour for a good few of us. (feature)

'De jour' is baffling – neither French nor recognised franglais. Should it
be 'de rigueur'?

> 'It reminded me of the wonderful films noir . . .' (column)

'Noir' should be 'noirs' (to agree with films).

> The Burberry check had become the ultimate symbol of nouveau
> rich naff. (feature)

'Rich' (English) should be 'riche' (French).

> When it opened in 1992, my play Oleanna was a *succès de scandal*, a
> handy French phrase meaning everyone was so enraged by it that
> everyone had to see it. (feature by playwright David Mamet)

The handy French phrase is in fact 'succès de scandale' (scandal being
English).

> It is considered de classé to make distinctions within low-brow culture.
> (column)

'De classé' should be 'déclassé'.

> If the woman could make pigeon fois gras . . . (column)

'Fois' (time) should be 'foie' (liver).

> Couples were squabbling over whether to have moules marinieres with
> garlic butter . . . (feature)

'Marinieres' should be 'marinière' (short for 'à la marinière').

> There are 14 English restaurants in the world top 50, the same number
> as provided by those self-appointed custodians of haute and bas
> cuisine, France and Italy, put together. (feature)

'Bas' should be 'basse' (to agree with cuisine, as haute does).

> Too high, if you believe what Hutton himself is said to have told
> confidantes. (feature)

Why 'confidantes' not 'confidants'? Does Hutton speak only to women?

> A former technical college awarded full university status in 1966, Aston
> was the surprise debutante in the Top 20 of this year's Guardian
> university league tables. (feature)

'Debutante' should be 'debutant' since universities are not feminine.

> As well as entrée-sized salads, McDonalds introduced all white meat
> Chicken McNuggets . . . (feature)

This, written in New York but published in a London newspaper, will
be misunderstood by many readers whose 'entrée' is their first, not their
main, course.

> According to the Old Testament, on the other hand, anyone who so
> much as glimpses a parent *en déshabillé* should promptly be stoned to
> death. (book review)

The writer wants 'en déshabillé' to mean naked but in French it means
partly dressed.

> A wife whose 'rack', as certain Americans are pleased to call an
> *embonpoint*, he refers to openly as 'the franchise'. 'At age 34, her
> breasts still had market value . . .' (book review)

So we're talking about a woman's breasts. But the English reviewer shoots
himself in the foot by objecting to 'rack' and 'franchise' in the name of
'embonpoint', a pretentious misuse (it means a fat tummy).

11
Figures

Figures are a minefield for journalists. Some find simple arithmetic difficult. Others, having grasped the point of a story involving figures, seem determined to inflict every minor detail on the reader. Journalists often exaggerate the importance of anything to do with figures and fail to apply their critical faculties to claims based on them.

What cannot be overstated is the need for journalists to be numerate as well as literate. Figures, after all, are facts expressed in numerical terms. If you cannot understand percentages, how can you expect to write an accurate story about them?

If, in 2006, 20 per cent of British people go to the cinema at least once, and in 2007, 25 per cent go, that is *not* an increase of 5 per cent. It is an increase of a quarter of 20 per cent – that is, an increase of 25 per cent.

Here I have deliberately gone back a stage from the percentage to the fraction to make the point easier to understand. When writing a story, though, you should not mix different ways of expressing figures – percentages and fractions, say – to make the copy more interesting to read. The effect will be confusion.

Percentages and probabilities can be very misleading in health stories. Say that out of 100 men in their 50s with normal cholesterol, four will be expected to have a heart attack, whereas out of 100 men of the same age with high cholesterol, six will be expected to have a heart attack. That's either two more than four, so an increase of 50 per cent, or it's two more out of 100, so an increase of 2 per cent – either a dramatic increase or a modest one. It makes more sense to communicate risk by using normal numbers than percentages.

If a typical basket of goods costs £1 in year one, £1.10 a year later and £1.20 a year after that, then a retail price index of 100 in year one will be 110 in year two and 120 in year three. The index has risen by 10 points in both years. This is how changes in stock market indexes, where the goods in the basket are shares, are usually reported.

Changes in retail prices tend to be reported in terms of percentage change. For the basket in our example the index has risen by 10 per cent from year one to year two, but the increase from year two to year three is a little under 9.1 per cent – the result of dividing 10p (the increase in price) by £1.10 (the price at the start of the year) and then multiplying by 100. The percentage increase in retail prices is one measure of inflation.

Note that although prices have risen in both years of the example – and by exactly the same cash amount – the rate of inflation has *fallen* in the second year.

Always remember that figures can be interpreted in different ways. Suppose that a survey appears to show that one road accident in four is alcohol-related. In following up the story it may be worth considering the point that – apparently – three accidents in four are *not* alcohol-related.

Be sceptical about polls. Before writing a story based on an opinion poll ask yourself what the questions asked really mean.

All polls based on a sample are subject to what statisticians call a margin of error and other people might call variability in their results. If a poll is repeated, the results will be different each time, even if not a single person changes their views.

In a typical political poll where the real answer is that half the population take a particular view, impeccable pollsters will find that most of the time their results show the figure to be between 47 per cent and 53 per cent with a tendency towards the 50 mark. Thus two polls taken a month apart could report a 6 per cent difference without anybody changing their mind. Similarly, two polls showing a figure of 50 per cent could be describing populations where the true figures were 47 and 53 per cent.

So it makes little sense for journalists to make big stories out of small changes in what the polls are showing.

Even perfectly managed polls will sometimes produce results that lie outside the typical 3 per cent margin of error. This is not an accident: it is exactly what statistics expects. Results like these are often called 'rogue polls'. It is when you get a rogue poll – crying out for sensational treatment because the results are so dramatic – that you need to be most cautious.

Percentage swing is the number of people in a hundred changing sides. If 7 per cent of the population switch from party A to party B, the swing is 7 per cent to party B. Party B's vote goes up 7 per cent and party A's down 7 per cent, so the gap between the parties changes by 14 per cent. That's why it takes only a 7 per cent swing to overturn a 14 per cent majority.

Take care with averages. An average tends to be somewhere in the middle of a set of figures. It is not news to write:

> Almost 50 per cent of British people have shorter than average holidays.

So too with the IQ scale whose midpoint is 100 – about half of us must have an IQ score lower than 100.

Avoid such technical terms as 'mean', 'median' and 'percentile' unless you are writing for a technical journal.

In general, percentages are harder to cope with than fractions – and fractions are harder than whole numbers. So wherever possible say 'one person in 10' rather than '10 per cent' or 'one tenth'.

With money prefer whole figures to decimals – £900,000 not £0.9m – but prefer decimals to fractions. In English decimals take a full point: 12.5. And, except in technical journals, figures greater than 999 take commas: 1,000.

In the house style of most publications figures start at 10 – but avoid mixing figures and words: write '9–10 people' not 'nine-10'.

Never start a sentence – still less a paragraph – with a figure since it looks ugly and creates typographical problems. So instead of:

> '14 people died when . . .'

write:

> 'Fourteen people died when . . .'

Don't solve the problem by writing:

> 'About 14 people died when . . .'

Indeed always avoid approximating precise figures as in:

> 'About 43.3 per cent'/'Around 123 people'

And don't use such phrases as 'a substantial number', 'a significant minority', 'a large proportion', 'a high percentage of the population': they are empty words pretending to be impressive and/or precise.

Get dates right. 'Between' must be followed by 'and'; 'from' by 'to'. Do not write 'between 1914–18' or 'from 1914–1918'. Instead write either 'in 1914–18' or 'between 1914 and 1918' or 'from 1914 to 1918'. That makes it possible to write:

> German rearmament took place between 1914–18 and 1939–45.

Should it be first/firstly, second/secondly? The shorter form is preferable but there is nothing wrong with the longer form – check your house style.

The British billion was once worth a million million. Now, as in the United States, it is worth only a thousand million.

Figures are hard to read. Do not litter your copy with them – unless you are writing for a technical journal. Even there, consider taking most of the figures out of the copy and putting them in a box or table.

Finally, do use a calculator to check figures – don't take other people's arithmetic on trust.

Appendix
Bulletin style guide

Bulletin 16/24 is a local email newsletter circulating in the Charente and Dordogne departments of France.

a (not an) historian, hotel etc (but **an** heir, honour etc)
- omit a/an from the titles of organisations (but not books etc)

abbreviations: units of measure are abbreviated and set close-up: a 30m drop, 120kph, a 5kg hammer. But distances and sums of money are not: he fell 20 metres; it cost £1 million.
- Most organisations should be written out in full when first mentioned (the World Health Organisation), then abbreviated (the WHO) but note: the BBC, the IRA.
- Some titles are cumbersome so prefer BSE, mad cow disease; the Gaullist party, the RPR.
- Abbreviations do not take a full point.
  see also **acronyms**

accents: keep accents on words of French origin to distinguish résumé from resume, pâté from pate etc

achilles heel/tendon (no cap or apostrophe)

acknowledgement (not acknowledgment)

acronyms: some abbreviations are spoken and written as words with initial cap: Nato, Aids

adaptation (not adaption)

addenda is the plural of addendum

adrenalin (not adrenaline)

adviser (not advisor) but **advisory**

affect (to influence) is confused with **effect** (to accomplish)

ageing (not aging)

agendas is the plural of agenda

aggravate: use to mean make worse, not annoy

aircraft/airplane (not aeroplane)

alibi: use to mean being elsewhere, not excuse

all right (not alright)

Americanisms: write in British English (lift not elevator, pavement not sidewalk, envisage not envision) but note that usage is changing: modern British children are raised more often than brought up and usually play with toy trucks rather than lorries

amid (not amidst)

amok (not amuck)

among (not amongst)

ampersand (&): use only in company names

answerphone: *see also* **trade names** p. 161

anticipate: make use of in advance/expect – don't use

apostrophes: words like men, women and children are plural so the apostrophe goes before the s: children's. In names of places and organisations follow their practice unless it is obviously illiterate: so write Siddalls, Sainsbury's but never womens or womens'. Add an extra s after the apostrophe only if it is sounded: St Thomas's but achilles heel/tendon

appendixes is the plural of appendix (both in books and in the body)

approx(imately): use **about**

arguably: possibly/probably – don't use

around: use **about**

artist (not artiste)

assure (to give confidence to) is confused with **ensure** (to make happen) and **insure** (to arrange insurance)

bail (court, cricket)/**bail out** (company, water from boat)

bale (straw)/**bale out** (of airplane)

balk (not baulk)

barbecue (not barbeque, bar-b-q)

beaus is the plural of beau (meaning boyfriend)

beg the question: *see* **clichés**

benefited (not benefitted)

biased (not biassed)

block (not bloc)

blond(e): women are blonde(s); men are blond; women and men have blond hair

bogey (one over par at golf)/**bogie** (railway trolley)/**bogy** (goblin)

bored: by/with (not of)

Brit: don't use

bureaus is the plural of bureau (desk) but **bureaux** is the plural of bureau (office)

burnt (not burned)

bused/busing (not bussed/bussing)

Canute (King): *see* **clichés**

canvas (paint)/**canvass** (for votes)

CAPS/lower case: always prefer lower case – second world war, prime minister

capsize is an exception to the -ise rule

caviar (not caviare)

celibate: unmarried/abstaining from sex – don't use (except in vow of celibacy)

censor (prevent publication) is confused with **censure** (criticise)

centre: in/on (not around/round)

château(x): include circumflex

chauvinist: absurdly nationalistic/sexist – use with care

chronic: use to mean recurrent, not 'very bad'

clichés: try to avoid using them. Never use the ones that people generally get wrong, eg beg the question, the curate's egg, Frankenstein, Hobson's choice and King Canute

cohort: group of people/individual colleague – don't use

collective nouns take either singular or plural verbs (the team is/are) but don't change suddenly from one to the other

combat (verb)/**combated/ing** (not combatted/ing) – but use only in quotes: otherwise use fight/fought/fighting

commence: use **begin** or **start**

compare to (for something completely different – Shall I compare thee to a summer's day?) is confused with **compare with** (like with like – last year's figures with this year's)

conjunctions can start sentences. And this is an example. But don't overdo it.
- If you start a sentence with a conjunction like because or while, make it a complete sentence with a main clause, so avoid the following example. Because it's ungrammatical.

connection (not connexion)

contemporary: belonging to the same time/modern – use with care

continual (recurring with breaks) is confused with **continuous** (without a break)

courtesy titles: don't use Mr, Mrs, Miss, Ms, Mme, Mlle. Call people John Smith or Marie Duval the first time you refer to them, then John/Marie or Smith/Duval according to context

criteria is the plural of criterion

curate's egg: *see* **clichés**

currently: use **now**

cut (noun – not cutback) but to cut back

cuttings (press – not clippings)

data: use as both singular (not datum) and plural

dates: 20 March 1942 (no th or commas); the 1960s (no apostrophe)
- Don't combine from or between with a dash: write from 1940 to 1945, between 1940 and 1945 or 1940–45, not from 1940–45 or between 1940–1945

decimate: kill 1 in 10/destroy large numbers – don't use

deserts (runs away, sandy places, what is deserved) is confused with **desserts** (puddings)

détente: include accent

dexterous (not dextrous)

dicy (not dicey)

dice: use as both singular (not die) and plural

differ/different: use *from*, not *to* or *than*

dike (not dyke)

dilemma: use to mean awkward choice between two, not problem

discreet (prudent) is confused with **discrete** (separate)

disinterested: impartial/bored – don't use

disk for computers, **disc** for everything else

dispatch (not despatch)

dissociate (not disassociate)

dos and don'ts: only one apostrophe

dotcom (not dot-com, dot.com)

double negatives: avoid both the comic-colloquial (I don't know nothing about it) and the pompous (I am not unmindful of your wishes)

draft (sketch, money order)/**draught** (beer, depth for ships)

dreamt (not dreamed)

due to: must follow a noun or pronoun as in 'The cancellation was due to bad weather'. Instead of 'The train was cancelled due to bad weather' write 'The train was cancelled because of bad weather'

duffel (not duffle)

dwarfs (not dwarves) is the plural of dwarf

dying (a death)/**dyeing** (a jumper)

economic (about economics)/**economical** (thrifty)

effect: *see* **affect**

eg: comma before but not after

egregious: distinguished/notorious – don't use

email (not e-mail)

encyclopedia (not encyclopaedia)

ensure: *see* **assure**

envisage (not envision)

etc: no commas, no full stop

expatriate (not ex-patriot – unless they've stopped loving their country)

expat: don't use

fed up: with (not of)

fetus (not foetus)

fewer/less: if there are fewer trees there will be less wood

figures: *see* **numbers**

flaunt (display) is confused with **flout** (treat with contempt)

focused/focusing (not focussed/focussing)

folk, meaning people, also has the plural form folks; for the possessive use folks' (old folks' home)

following: if you mean after, use after

forbear (abstain)/**forebear** (ancestor)

forceful (energetic) is confused with **forcible** (done by force)

foreign words: *see* **franglais**. In general avoid words from other languages except French; if you have to use a non-French word, put it into italics. Don't put French words into italics

forego (go before)/**forgo** (do without)

format(verb)/**formatted**/**formatting**: use only for computers

formulas is the plural of formula

franglais: avoid misuses of French in English (eg embonpoint, which does not mean ample bosom) but, if appropriate, use French words that are current among local English-speaking people (eg bâche for tarpaulin, hangar for shed)

Frankenstein: *see* **clichés**

freelance (not freelancer)

further (not farther, even for distance)

gaff (hook to catch a fish, room or flat)/**gaffe** (blunder)

gay: use to mean homosexual, not light-hearted

geezer (bloke)/**geyser** (spring)

gender: *see* **sex**

geriatric: use to mean relating to care of the old, not old

graffiti is the plural of graffito

grey (not gray)

grisly (horrible)/**grizzly** (kind of bear)

handkerchiefs is the plural of handkerchief

hangar (shed)/**hanger** (for clothes)

hello (not hallo, hullo)

hiccup (not hiccough)

historic (famous)/**historical** (about history)

hi-tech (not high-tech)

hoard (hidden stock)/**horde** (multitude)

Hobson's choice: *see* **clichés**

hoi polloi (the plebs): don't use

holy (sacred)/**holey** (full of holes)

hopefully: by all means travel hopefully but don't write 'Hopefully we'll arrive tomorrow'

hurrah (not hooray) but Hooray Henry

hyphens: use them to make meaning clear: extra-marital sex; a black-cab driver/black cab-driver; a close-knit group. Do not use after -ly adverbs: instead prefer a closely knit group. When you hyphenate to mark word breaks, avoid a succession of hyphens and break words into their constituent parts. Avoid unintentional words, eg anal-ysis

I/me: prefer 'Fred and I were there' to 'Fred and me were there'; 'It's me' to 'It is I'; 'between you and me' to 'between you and I'

ie: comma before but not after; no full stops

imply (suggest) is confused with **infer** (deduce)

inchoate: unformed/incoherent – don't use

infer: *see* **imply**

infinitives may be split by adverbs if necessary (It's difficult to really get to know somebody) but always ask yourself whether the adverb is necessary

initials: use people's first names unless they are publicly known by their initials; then set them in caps without full points or spaces: PD James. But note: ee cummings; kd lang

inquire/y (not enquire/y)

install/installation/instalment

instil/instillation/instilment

insure: *see* **assure**

-ise (not -ize) in all words except **capsize**

italics: use for the titles of newspapers, periodicals, books, plays, films, one-off broadcasts, serials and series. In newspaper titles 'The' stays in roman type, lower case, with the town or city of publication included for clarity: the London *Times*, the New York *Times*, the Portsmouth *News*, etc. In periodical titles 'The' stays in roman type, lower case: the *Economist*, the *Journalist*. All other titles are given in full: *The Merchant of Venice*
  - Also use italics *rarely* (rather than caps or screamers) for emphasis.
  - Also *see* **foreign words**

jail (not gaol)

jargon: try to translate technical terms into English

jewellery (not jewelry)

John o'Groat's: keep the second apostrophe (it was originally John o'Groat's House)

judgment (not judgement)

laisser-faire (not laissez-faire)

lay/lie: lay the table and lie on the floor

leapt (not leaped)

learnt (as verb – not learned)

lend, to not to loan

less: *see* **fewer**

leukemia (not leukaemia)

lie: *see* **lay**

like: distinguish between the following:

1   like used to compare: Fruit trees are like flowers: they need water. Where appropriate, use commas to mark a parenthesis: Fruit trees, like flowers, need water.

2   like used instead of such as – don't use commas: Fruit trees like the cherry need pruning.

3   like used as a pause word in colloquial quotes (nowhere else) – do use commas: 'I'm, like, a singer'. (The speaker means they are a singer: take the commas away and it becomes a comparison.)

likeable (not likable)

linage (payment by the line)/**lineage** (ancestry)

linchpin (not lynchpin)

lovable (not loveable)

mantel/mantelpiece (above the fireplace)/**mantle** (cloak)

marijuana (not marihuana)

masterful (dominating) is confused with **masterly** (skilful)

may/might: 'First aid may have saved him' means that he may be alive. To show that we know he's dead, it must be: First aid might have saved him.

me: *see* **I**

media is the plural of medium meaning, eg the press

medieval (not mediaeval)

mediums is the plural of medium meaning spiritualist

metal (such as gold)/**mettle** (courage)

meter (gauge)/**metre** (measure)

might: *see* **may**

mileage (not milage)

militate (contend) is confused with **mitigate** (soften)

movable (not moveable except in Hemingway's 'A Moveable Feast')

Muslim (not Moslem)

naivety (not naiveté)

no one: not no-one

none takes either a singular or a plural verb; the plural often sounds more natural: 'None of our problems have been solved'

nosy (not nosey)

numbers: one to nine are written as words and figures start at 10; but 9–10, not nine-10
  • Percentages are always in figures: 6.5 per cent; 1 per cent
  • For time use the 24-hour clock: the meeting will be at 18h/18h30
  • Figures above 999 take commas: 1,760
  • Decimals take a full point: 17.6

OK (not okay)

only should go as near as possible to the word or phrase it refers to: 'She arrived only last week. But we can live with 'I'm only here for the beer'

orientate (not orient)

paediatrician/paedophile (not pediatrician/pedophile)

participles: when dangling, watch your participles. This is the commonest – and worst – mistake in modern journalism. 'Born in Brixton, his father was a trapeze artist.' Who?

pedaller (cyclist)/**pedlar** (hawker)/**peddler** (drug dealer)

people is mainly used as the plural of person (the people's champion) but it is also used as a singular noun to mean nation; then its plural is peoples (possessive peoples')

phenomena is the plural of phenomenon

phoney (not phony)

prepositions can end sentences – what else are you thinking of?

prescribe (lay down) is confused with **proscribe** (prohibit)

pressurise (not pressure) as verb

prevaricate (evade the truth) is confused with **procrastinate** (defer action)

preventive (not preventative)

pricy (not pricey)

principal (main or head)/**principle** (basis)

pristine: original/new – don't use

processor (not processer)

procrastinate: *see* **prevaricate**

program for computers, **programme** for everything else

proscribe: *see* **prescribe**

protagonist: chief actor/any person or character/person in favour – don't use

protester (not protestor)

queries (question marks): include after rhetorical questions

quotes: in text use single quotes with double inside single; in headlines use single quotes
- Please don't start stories with quotes
- Introduce full-sentence quotes with a colon not a comma
- Edit quotes when necessary (a) to shorten (b) to clarify (c) to remove bad grammar, but *never* change the meaning

race: only mention race where it is relevant; in general use the descriptions people use of themselves. Terms include Afro-Caribbean, Asian, black, mixed race, Romany, white
- In general use caps for geographically based terms; but distinguish between Gypsy for specific groups of Romany people and gypsy for general references to an outdoor, unconventional way of life

realise (not realize)

rebut: deny, argue against, show to be false – don't use

redundancy/repetition/saying it twice/tautology: whatever you call it don't write 'They were both talking to each other'

refute: deny, show to be false – don't use

register (not registry) **office** for marriage

regularly: use to mean at regular intervals, not often

relative/relation (for family): use either – but not both close together

religion: use caps for Anglican, Baptist, Buddhist, Catholic (not Roman Catholic), Christian, Jewish, Muslim, Protestant etc
- Give Anglican clerics their courtesy title the first time you refer to them: the Rev John/Mary Smith. Then call them John/Mary or Smith according to context; never call anyone the Rev Smith

repetition: see **redundancy**

reticent: use to mean reluctant to speak, not reluctant to act

review (critical notice)/**revue** (theatrical show)

rise (in prices – not hike)

saying it twice: *see* **redundancy**

screamers (! ! !): avoid

sensual (physically gratifying) is confused with **sensuous** (affecting the senses)

sex/gender: gender is a grammatical term; to distinguish between men and women prefer the word sex
- Don't use male terms generically: say police officers not policemen, firefighters not firemen. But for individuals use spokesman/spokeswoman, chairman/chairwoman; don't use spokesperson, chairperson etc
- For female actors use actress – also abbess, countess, duchess, goddess, marchioness – but not poetess, sculptress etc

singing (a song)/**singeing** (a beard)

smelt (not smelled)

smidgen (not smidgeon)

spelling: use British not American spelling
- For words not given in this style guide follow Chambers (not Collins, Longmans, Oxford, Penguin and certainly not Webster's), using the first spelling given

spelt (not spelled)

spicy (not spicey)

spoilt (not spoiled)

stadiums is the plural of stadium

story (tale)/**storey** (in building)

straitjacket (not straightjacket)

sufficient: use enough

swap (not swop)

swinging (from a tree)/**swingeing** (savage)

tautology: *see* **redundancy**

that/which: This is the house that Jack built (defines, no commas); Jack's house, which he bought last year, is worth £1 million (adds extra information, commas)

they is better than he/she and he or she if the sex of the person is not specified: Anyone can come if they want to

tortuous (difficult) is confused with **torturous** (like torture)

trade (not trades) **union** but **Trades Union Congress**

trade names: unless a trade name is important to the story, always use an equivalent term, eg vacuum cleaner for Hoover, ballpoint pen for Biro, photocopier for Xerox (see list of trade names below)

transatlantic (not transAtlantic)

tsar (not czar)

T-shirt (not tee-shirt)

tyre (not tire)

verbal: use to mean spoken (as in verbal agreement)

wagon (not waggon)

wagons-lits is the plural of wagon-lit

waiver (renunciation)/**waver** (vacillate)

which: *see* **that**

while (not whilst)

whisky (not whiskey – unless Irish or American is specified)

who/whom: in general prefer 'Who did you invite?' to 'Whom did you invite?' Never write 'Whom did you say was there?'

Trade names

adidas (lower-case a): sportswear

Ansafone: answering machine

Aspro: aspirin analgesic

Autocue: teleprompter

Biro: ballpoint pen

Burberry: mackintosh

Calor: bottled gas
Caterpillar: continuous-tread vehicle
Cellophane: cellulose film
Coca-Cola: cola drink
Courtelle: acrylic fibre
Crimplene: polyester filament yarn

Dacron: polyester fibre
Dettol: antiseptic disinfectant
Dictaphone: dictating machine
Dinky: miniature toy vehicle
Distalgesic: analgesic
Dolby: noise-reduction circuitry
Dormobile: minibus
Dralon: acrylic fibre
Dunlopillo: resilient foam
Dymo: embossing tool, tape

Elastoplast: sticking plaster

Fibreglass: glass fibre
Flymo: hover mower
Formica: laminate

Hoover: vacuum cleaner

Instamatic: cartridge camera

Jacuzzi: whirlpool bath
Jiffy bag: postal bag

KiloStream: digital communications
Kleenex: paper tissues

Land Rover: all-purpose vehicle
Lego: interlocking toy bricks
Letraset: dry transfer lettering
Levi's: jeans

Meccano: assembly-kit toy
MegaStream: digital communications

Nescafé: instant coffee

Orlon: acrylic fibre

Pentothal: barbiturate for anaesthesia
Perspex: acrylic sheet
Photostat: photocopier/y
Plasticine: modelling clay
Polaroid: filter, camera, sunglasses
Portakabin: portable building
Primus: stove, heater
Pyrex: heat-resistant glass

Range Rover: all-purpose vehicle

Scotch Tape: transparent adhesive tape
Sellotape: transparent adhesive tape
Spam: chopped pork and ham

Teflon: non-stick coating on pans
Terylene: polyester fibre
Thermos: vacuum flask
Triplex: safety glass

Vaseline: petroleum jelly
Velcro: press-together fastening

Xerox: photocopier

Yellow Pages: business telephone directory

Glossary of terms used in journalism

Journalism is rich in jargon. Some of it comes from printing (book for magazine); or survives from the pre-computer age (spike for rejected copy); or is imported from the United States (clippings for cuttings). It is often punchy and graphic (ambush, bust, fireman). But if it crops up in copy (eg in stories about the media) the sub will usually have to change it (replace 'story' by 'report') or explain it (after 'chapel' insert 'office branch' in brackets). The obvious exception is in publications for journalists such as *Press Gazette* and the *Journalist*.

ABC: Audit Bureau of Circulations – source of independently verified circulation figures

ad: advertisement

add: extra copy to add to existing story

advance: 1 text of speech or statement issued to journalists beforehand; 2 expenses paid before a trip

advertorial: advertisement presented as editorial

agencies: news agencies, eg PA and Reuters

agony column: regular advice given on personal problems sent in by readers; hence agony aunt

ambush: journalists lying in wait for unsuspecting, unwilling interviewee

ampersand: & – symbol for 'and'

angle: particular approach to story, journalist's point of view in writing it

art editor: visual journalist responsible for design and layout of publication

artwork: illustrations (eg drawings, photographs) prepared for reproduction

ascender: the part of a lower-case letter (eg b and d) that sticks out above the x-height in a typeface

attribution: identifying the journalist's source of information or quote

author's (corrections, marks): proof corrections by writer of story

back number, issue: previous issue of publication

back of the book: second part of magazine (after the centre spread)

backbench, the: senior newspaper journalists who make key production decisions

backgrounder: explanatory feature to accompany news story

bad break: clumsy hyphenation at the end of a line

banner (headline): one in large type across front page

basket: where copy goes – once a physical basket, now a digital folder

bastard measure: type set to a width that is not standard for the page

beard: the space between a letter and the edge of the base on which it is designed

beat: American term for specialist area covered by reporter

bill(board): poster promoting edition of newspaper, usually highlighting main news story

black: duplicate of written story (from colour of carbon paper once used with typewriter)

bleed: (of an image) go beyond the type area to the edge of a page

blob: solid black circle used for display effect or to tabulate lists

blob par: extra paragraph introduced by blob

blow up: enlarge (part of) photograph

blown quote: another term for pull quote

blurb: displayed material promoting contents of another page or future issue

body copy: the main text of a story, as opposed to page furniture

body type: the main typeface in which a story is set (as opposed to display)

bold: thick black type, used for emphasis

book: printer's (and so production journalist's) term for magazine

bot: black on tone

box: copy enclosed by rules to give it emphasis and/or separate it from the main text

breaker: typographical device, eg crosshead, used to break up text on the page

brief: 1 short news item; 2 instruction to journalist on how to approach story

bring up: bring forward part of story to earlier position

broadsheet: large-format newspaper

bromide: photographic print

bullet (point): another term for blob

bureau: office of news agency or newspaper office in foreign country

business-to-business: current term for what were once called 'trade' magazines, ie those covering a business area, profession, craft or trade

bust: (of a headline) be too long for the space available

buy-up interview: exclusive bought by publication

byline: writer's name as it appears in print at the beginning of a story

c & lc: capital and lower-case letters

call out: another term for pull quote

calls (also check calls): routine phone calls made by reporters to organisations such as police and fire brigade to see if a story is breaking

camera-ready: (eg artwork) prepared for reproduction

caps: capital letters

caption: words used with a picture (usually underneath), identifying where necessary and relating it to the accompanying story

caption story: extension of picture caption into a self-contained story

cast off: estimate amount of printed matter copy would make

casual: journalist employed by the shift

catch(line): short word (not printed) identifying different elements of a story in the editorial process

centre: set type with equal space on either side

centre spread: middle opening of tabloid or magazine

chapel: office branch of media union (the shop steward is the father, FoC, or mother, MoC, of the chapel)

character: unit of measurement for type including letters, figures, punctuation marks and spaces

chequebook journalism: paying large sums for stories

chief sub: senior subeditor in charge of the others

city desk: financial section of British national newspaper (in the US the city desk covers home news)

classified advertising: small ads 'classified' by subject matter, grouped in a separate section

clippings/clips: American term for cuttings

close quotes: end of section in direct quotes

close up: reduce space between lines, words or characters

CMYK: cyan, magenta, yellow and black, the process (basic printing) colours

col: column

colour piece: news story written as feature with emphasis on journalist's reactions

colour sep(aration)s: method by which the four process colours (CMYK) are separated from a colour original

column: 1 standard vertical division of page; 2 regular feature by journalist often encouraged to be opinionated and/or entertaining

column rule: light rule between columns of type

conference: meeting of editorial staff to plan current/next issue

consumer magazines: the category includes specialist titles (eg *Angling Times*), women's magazines and those of general interest

contact sheet: photographer's sheet of small prints

contacts book: a journalist's list of contacts with details of phone, fax, email, etc

contents bill: *see* bill

controlled circulation: free distribution of specialist title to target readership by geography (free newspapers) or interest group (business-to-business magazines)

copy: text of story

copy taster: *see* taster

copyright: right to reproduce original material

copytaker: telephone typist who takes down copy from reporter

corr: correspondent

correction: published statement correcting errors in story

correspondent: journalist covering specialist area, eg education

coverlines: selling copy on front cover

credit (line): name of photographer or illustrator as it appears in print next to their work

Cromalins: the Dupont system of glossy colour proofs

crop: cut (image) to size or for better effect

crosshead: line or lines, taken from the text, set bigger and bolder than the body type and inserted between paragraphs to liven up page

cut: shorten or delete copy

cut-out: illustration with background masked, painted or cut to make it stand out on the page

cuts: cuttings

cuttings: stories taken (originally cut) from newspapers and filed electronically under subject

cuttings job: story that is over-dependent on cuttings

dateline: place from which copy is filed

deadline: time story (or any part of it) is due

deck: originally one of a series of headlines stacked on top of each other; now usually used to mean one line of a headline

delayed drop: device in news story of delaying important facts for effect

delete: remove

descender: the part of a lower-case letter (eg g and j) that sticks out below the x-height in a typeface

desk: newspaper department, eg picture desk

deskman: American term for male subeditor

diary, the: list of news events to be covered; hence an off-diary story is one originated by the reporter

diary column: gossip column

direct input: transmission of copy direct from the journalist's keyboard to the computer for typesetting (as opposed to the old system in which compositors retyped copy)

disclaimer: statement explaining that a particular person or organisation was not the subject of a previously published story

display ads: ordinary (not 'classified') ads which appear throughout a publication

display type: type for headlines etc

district reporter: one covering a particular area away from the main office

doorstepping: reporters lying in wait for (usually) celebrities outside their homes

double: a story published twice in the same issue of a publication

double-column: (of text, headline, illustration) across two columns

double (page) spread: two facing pages in a magazine, whether advertising or editorial

downtable subs: those other than the chief sub and deputies

drop cap, letter: outsize initial capital letter used to start story or section; it drops down alongside the text which is indented to accommodate it

drop quotes: outsize quotes used to mark quoted matter

dummy: 1 pre-publication edition of new publication used to sell advertising and experiment editorially; 2 blank version of publication, eg to show quality and weight of paper; 3 complete set of page proofs

edition: version of newspaper printed for particular circulation area or time

editor: senior journalist responsible for publication or section

editorial: 1 leading article expressing editorial opinion; 2 content that is not advertising

editor's conference: main planning meeting for next issue

em, en: units of measurement for type – the width of the two letters m and n

embargo: time before which an organisation supplying material, eg by press release, does not want it published

ends: the story ends here

EPD: electronic picture desk

EPS file: Encapsulated PostScript file

exclusive: claim by publication that it has a big story nobody else has

exes: journalists' out-of-pocket expenses

face: type design

facing matter: (of advertising) opposite editorial

facsimile: exact reproduction, as with electronic transmission of pages

feature: article that goes beyond reporting of facts to explain and/or entertain; also used of any editorial material that is not news or listings; hence feature writer, features editor

file: transmit copy

filler: short news item to fill space

fireman: traditional term for reporter sent to trouble spot when story breaks

fit: (of copy etc) to occupy exactly the space available

flannel panel: magazine's address, contact information and list of staff

flash: brief urgent message from news agency

flatplan: page-by-page plan of issue

flip: (of picture) transpose left to right

flush left or right: (of type) having one consistent margin with the other ragged

fold, the: centre fold in a newspaper so that only the upper half of the paper ('above the fold') is visible at the point of sale

folio: page (number)

follow up: take published story as the starting point for an update

format: 1 size, shape or style of publication or section; 2 computer instruction; hence to format

fount (pronounced font and now often spelt that way): typeface

free(sheet): free newspaper

freebie: something useful or pleasant, often a trip, supplied free to journalists

freelance: self-employed journalist who sells material to various outlets

freelancer: American term for freelance

fudge: another term for stop press

full out: (of type) not indented

galley proof: typeset proof not yet made up into a page

gatefold: an extra page which folds out from a magazine

ghost writer: journalist writing on behalf of someone else, often by interviewing them; hence to ghost (eg a column)

gone to bed: passed for press so too late for corrections

grams per square metre (gsm; g/m2): the measure used to define the weight of paper

graphics: visual material, usually drawn

grid: design skeleton specifying (eg) number and width of columns

gutter: space between two facing pages; can also be used of space between columns

H & J: (of copy on screen) hyphenated and justified, so in the form in which it will be typeset

hack, hackette: jocular terms for journalist

hair space: thinnest space between typeset letters

half-tone: illustration broken into dots of varying sizes

handout: printed material, eg press release, distributed to journalists

hanging indent: copy set with first line of each paragraph full out and subsequent ones indented

hard copy: copy on paper, eg printout, rather than screen

head, heading: headline

heavy: broadsheet newspaper
heavy type: thicker than standard
hold (over): keep material for future use
hot metal: old typesetting system in which type was cast from molten metal
house ad: publisher's advertisement in its own publication
house journal: publication for employees of a particular organisation
house style: the way a publication chooses to publish in matters of detail

imposition: arrangement of pages for printing
imprint: name and address of publisher and printer
in-house: inside a media organisation
in pro: in proportion (used of visual material to be reduced)
indent: set copy several characters in from left-hand margin
input: type copy into computer
insert: 1 extra copy to be included in existing story; 2 printed matter inserted in publication after printing and binding
intro: first paragraph of story; also used (confusingly) in some magazine offices to mean standfirst
ISDN: integrated services digital network – a means of transmitting editorial material between offices, to printers, etc
italics: italic (sloping) type

jack-line: another word for widow
journo: jocular term for journalist
justified: type set with consistent margins

kern: reduce the space between characters in typeset copy
kicker: introductory part of caption or headline
kill: drop a story; hence kill fee for freelance whose commissioned story is not used
knocking copy: story written with negative angle

label: (of headline) without a verb
landscape: horizontal picture
layout: arrangement of body type, headlines etc and illustrations on the page
lead: 1 main story on a page; 2 tip-off or idea for story (in the US the intro of a story is called the lead)
leader: leading article expressing editorial opinion
leader dots: three dots used to punctuate
leading (pronounced 'ledding'): space between lines (originally made by inserting blank slugs of lead between lines of type)
leg: column of typeset copy

legal: send material to be checked for legal problems, eg libel
legal kill: lawyer's instruction not to use
lensman: American term for male photographer
letter spacing: space between letters
libel: defamatory statement in permanent or broadcast form
lift: 1 use all or most of a story taken from one newspaper edition in the
    next; 2 steal a story from another media outlet and reproduce it with
    few changes
ligature: two or more joined letters
light face: type lighter than standard
linage (this spelling preferred to lineage): payment to freelances by the line;
    also refers to classified advertising without illustration
line drawing: drawing made up of black strokes
listings: lists of entertainment and other events with basic details
literal: typographical error
lobby, the: specialist group of political reporters covering parliament
local corr: local correspondent
logo: name, title or recognition word in particular design used on regular
    section or column; also used of magazine's front-page title
lower case: ordinary letters (not caps)

make-up: assembly of type and illustrations on the page ready for
    reproduction
mark up: specify the typeface, size and width in which copy is to be set
masking: covering part of photograph for reproduction
masthead: publication's front-page title
measure: width of typesetting
medium type: between light and heavy
merchandising: details of stockists and prices in consumer features
mf: more copy follows
model release: contract signed by photographic model authorising use of
    pictures
mono(chrome): printed in one colour, usually black
more: more copy follows
mug shot: photograph showing head (and sometimes shoulders)
must: copy that must appear, eg apology or correction
mutton: old name for an em

neg: photographic negative
news agency: supplier of news and features to media outlets
news desk: organising centre of newsroom
newsman: American term for male reporter
newsprint: standard paper on which newspapers are printed

newsroom: news reporters' room

nib: news in brief – short news item

night lawyer: barrister who reads newspaper proofs for legal problems

nose: intro of story; hence to renose – rewrite intro

NUJ: National Union of Journalists

nut: old name for an en; hence nutted, type indented one en

obit: obituary

off-diary: *see* diary, the

off-the-record: statements made to a journalist on the understanding that they will not be reported directly or attributed

on spec: uncommissioned (material submitted by freelance)

on-the-record: statements made to a journalist that can be reported and attributed

op-ed: feature page facing page with leading articles

open quotes: start of section in direct quotes

originals: photographs or other visual material for reproduction

orphan: first line of a paragraph at the foot of a page or column

out take: another term for pull quote

overlay: sheet of transparent paper laid over artwork with instructions on how to process it

overline: another word for strapline

overmatter: typeset material that does not fit the layout and must be cut

overprint: print over a previously printed background

PA: Press Association, Britain's national news agency

package: main feature plus sidebars

page furniture: displayed type, eg headlines, standfirsts and captions, used to project copy

page plan: editorial instructions for layout

page proof: proof of a made-up page

pagination: the number of pages in a publication; also a newspaper system's ability to make up pages

panel: another word for box

par, para: paragraph

paparazzo/i: photographer(s) specialising in pursuing celebrities

paste-up: page layout pasted into position

patch: specialist area covered by reporter

pay-off: final twist or flourish in the last paragraph of a story

peg: reason for publishing feature at a particular time

photomontage: illustration created by combining several photographs

pic, pix: press photograph(s)

pica: unit of type measurement

pick-up (of photographs): those that already exist and can therefore be picked up by journalists covering a story

picture desk: organising centre of collection and editing of pictures

piece: article

plate: printing image carrier from which pages are printed

point: 1 full stop; 2 standard unit of type size

pool: group of reporters sharing information and releasing it to other media organisations

PostScript: Adobe's page description language

PR(O): public relations (officer); hence someone performing a public relations role

press cuttings: *see* cuttings

press release: written announcement or promotional material by organisation sent to media outlets and individual journalists

profile: portrait in words of individual or organisation

proof: printout of part or whole of page so it can be checked and corrected

proofread: check proofs; hence proofreader

publisher: 1 publishing company; 2 individual in magazine publishing company with overall responsibility for title or group of titles

puff: story promoting person or organisation

pull: proof; to pull is to take a proof

pull (out) quote (blown quote, call out, out take): short extract from text set in larger type as part of page layout

pullout: separate section of publication that can be pulled out

pyramid: (usually inverted) conventional structure for news story with most important facts in intro

query: question mark

queue: collection of stories held in a computer

quote: verbatim quotation

quotes: quotation marks

ragged: (of type) with uneven margin

raised cap: outsize initial capital letter used to start story or section; it is raised above the text

range left or right: (of type) have one consistent margin with the other ragged

register: alignment of coloured inks on the printed page

rejig: rewrite copy, particularly in the light of later information

renose: rewrite intro of a story

reporter: gatherer and writer of news

repro house: company that processes colour pictures ready for printing

retainer: regular payment to local correspondent or freelance

retouch: alter photograph to emphasise particular feature

Reuters: international news agency

reverse indent: another term for hanging indent

reversed out: (type) printed in white on black or tinted background

revise: extra proof to check that corrections have been made

rewrite: write new version of story or section as opposed to subbing on copy

ring-round: story based on series of phone calls

river: white space running down a column of type, caused by space between words

roman: plain upright type

rough: sketch for layout

round-up: gathering of disparate elements for single story

RSI: repetitive strain injury, attributed to overuse and misuse of computer keyboard, mouse, etc

rule: line between columns or round illustrations

run: period of printing an edition or number of copies printed

run on: (of type) continue from one line, column or page to the next

running foot: title and issue date at the foot of the page

running head: title and issue date at the top of the page

running story: one that is constantly developing, over a newspaper's different editions or a number of days

running turns: pages with no paragraph breaks on first and last lines; also used of columns

rush: second most urgent message from news agency (after flash)

sans (serif): plain type (*see* serif) – this is an example

scaling (of pictures): calculating depth

schedule: 1 list of jobs for (eg) reporters; 2 publication's printing programme

scheme: make a plan of page layout

scoop: jocular word for exclusive

screamer: exclamation mark

screen: the number of dots per square inch of a half-tone

section: 1 separately folded part of newspaper; 2 complete printed sheet making up part of magazine

sell: another word for standfirst, often used in women's magazines

serif: decorative addition to type – this is an example

set and hold: typeset and keep for use later

setting: copy set in type

shift: daily stint worked by staff journalists and casuals

shoot: a photographic session

shy: (of headline) too short for the space available

sidebar: subsidiary story or other material placed next to main story, usually in box

sidehead: subsidiary heading, set flush left

sign-off: writer's name as it appears in print at the end of a story

sketch: light-hearted account of events, especially parliamentary

slip: newspaper edition for particular area or event

small caps: capital letters in smaller size of the same typeface

snap: early summary by news agency of important story to come

snapper: jocular term for press photographer

snaps: press photographs

solid: (of type) set without extra leading

spike: where rejected copy goes (originally a metal spike)

splash: newspaper's main front-page story

splash sub: subeditor responsible for tabloid's front page

spoiler: attempt by newspaper to reduce impact of rival's exclusive by publishing similar story

spot colour: second colour (after black) used in printing publication

spread: two facing pages

s/s: same size

standfirst: introductory matter accompanying headline, particularly used in features

stet: ignore deletion or correction (Latin for 'let it stand')

stone: bench where pages were made up; hence stone sub – subeditor who makes final corrections and cuts on page proofs

stop press: small area on back page of newspaper left blank for late news in days of hot metal

story: article, especially news report

strap(line): subsidiary headline above main headline

Street, the: Fleet Street, where many newspapers once had their offices

stringer: local correspondent; freelance on contract to a news organisation

style: house style

style book/style sheet: where house style is recorded

sub: subeditor

subhead: subsidiary headline

subtitle: another word for standfirst

tab(loid): popular small-format newspaper such as the *Sun*

tagline: explanatory note under headline

take: section of copy for setting

take back: (on proof) take words back to previous line

take over: (on proof) take words forward to next line

taster: production journalist who checks and selects copy; also coverline

think piece: feature written to show and provoke thought

tie-in: story connected with the one next to it

tint: shaded area on which type can be printed

tip(-off): information supplied (and usually paid for) whether by freelance or member of the public

titlepiece: traditional term for name of magazine as it appears on the cover – now replaced by masthead and logo

TOT: triumph over tragedy, feature formula particularly popular in women's magazines

tracking: space between characters

trade names: product names (eg Hoover, Kleenex, Velcro)

tranny: transparency – photograph in film form

trans(pose): reverse order

turn: part of story continued on a later page

typeface: a complete range of type in a particular style, eg Times New Roman

typescale: measuring rule for type

typo: American term for typographical error

typography: craft of using type

u/lc: upper and lower case

underscore: underline

unj(ustified): text set flush left, ragged right

upper and lower case: mixture of capitals and ordinary letters

upper case: capital letters

vignette: illustration whose edges gradually fade to nothing

vox pop: series of street interviews (Latin: *vox populi* – voice of the people)

weight: thickness or boldness of letters in a typeface

white space: area on page with no type or illustration

widow: single word or part of word at the end of a paragraph on a line by itself; originally the last line of a paragraph at the top of a page or column

wire: a means of transmitting copy by electronic signal; hence wire room

wob: white on black – type reversed out

wot: white on tone

x-height: height of the lower-case letters of a typeface (excluding ascenders and descenders)

Further reading

English usage and writing style

Amis, Kingsley, *The King's English*, HarperCollins, 1997

Blamires, Harry, *Correcting your English*, Bloomsbury, 1996

Bryson Bill, *Troublesome Words*, Viking, 2001

Burchfield R.W. (ed), *The New Fowler's Modern English Usage* (third edition), OUP, 1996

Burridge, Kate, *Blooming English*, ABC Books for the Australian Broadcasting Corporation, 2002

Cochrane James, *Between You and I*, Icon, 2003

Dummett, Michael, *Grammar and Style for Examination Candidates and Others*, Duckworth, 1993

Evans, Harold, *Essential English for Journalists, Editors and Writers*, revised by Crawford Gillan, Pimlico, 2000

Greenbaum, Sidney and Whitcut, Janet, *Longman Guide to English Usage*, Penguin, 1996

Gowers, Sir Ernest, *The Complete Plain Words* (second edition), revised by Sir Bruce Fraser, Pelican, 1977

Hicks, Wynford, *Quite Literally: Problem Words and How to Use Them*, Routledge, 2004

Humphrys, John, *Lost for Words*, Hodder, 2005

Mayes, Ian, *Only Correct: The Best of Corrections and Clarifications*, Guardian, 2005

Partridge, Eric, *You Have a Point There*, Routledge, 1990

—— *Usage and Abusage* (third edition), revised by Janet Whitcut, Penguin, 1999

Strunk, William, *The Elements of Style* (third edition), revised by E.B. White, Macmillan (New York), 1979, also available free at www.bartleby.com/141/

Trask, R.L., *Mind the Gaffe*, Penguin, 2001

Truss, Lynne, *Eats, Shoots & Leaves*, Profile, 2003

Waterhouse, Keith, *Waterhouse on Newspaper Style*, Viking, 1989

—— *English Our English*, Viking, 1991

House style

Austin, Tim (comp) *The Times Style and Usage Guide*, Collins 2003
  * updated online edition: www.timesonline.co.uk

The Economist Style Guide (eighth edition), Economist, 2003

Marsh, David and Marshall, Nikki (eds), *The Guardian Stylebook*, Guardian, 2004
  * updated online edition: www.guardian.co.uk

Ritter, R.M. (ed and comp), *New Oxford Dictionary for Writers and Editors*, OUP, 2005

Print journalism skills

Adams, Sally, *Interviewing for Journalists*, Routledge, 2001

Frost, Chris, *Reporting for Journalists*, Routledge, 2002

Hicks, Wynford, *Writing for Journalists*, Routledge, 1999

—— and Holmes, Tim, *Subediting for Journalists*, Routledge, 2002

Keeble, Richard, *Ethics for Journalists*, Routledge, 2001

McNae's Essential Law for Journalists, current edition, Butterworths

Mason, Peter and Smith, Derrick, *Magazine Law*, Routledge, 1998

Index

Related titles from Routledge

Writing for Broadcast Journalists

Rick Thompson

Writing for Broadcast Journalists guides readers through the differences between written and spoken language in journalism, helping broadcast journalists at every stage of their career to steer past such pitfalls as pronunciation, terms of address, and Americanized phrases, as well as to capitalize on the immediacy of the spoken word in writing broadcast news scripts.

Written in a lively and accessible style by an experienced BBC radio and TV journalist, *Writing for Broadcast Journalists* provides an invaluable guide to the techniques of writing for radio, television and online news sources. Sections include:

- guidance on tailoring your writing style to suit a particular broadcast news audience
- advice on editing agency copy
- tips on how to avoid clichés, 'news-speak' and Americanisms
- an appendix of 'dangerous' words and phrases, explaining correct usage and advising when to avoid certain terms.

ISBN 10: 0–415–31796–7 (hbk)
ISBN 10: 0–415–31797–5 (pbk)

ISBN 13: 9–78–0–415–31796–2 (hbk)
ISBN 13: 9–78–0–415–31797–9 (pbk)

Available at all good bookshops
For ordering and further information please visit:
www.routledge.com

Related titles from Routledge

Freelancing for Television and Radio

Leslie Mitchell

Freelancing for Television and Radio explains what it means to be a freelance in the world of the audio visual industries. From an outline of tax and employment issues it goes on to describe the ups and downs of the world in which the freelance works. Radio, television and related sectors like facilities and video production are assessed for the opportunities they offer the aspiring freelance, and there is also an analysis of the skills you need for a successful freelance career.

Freelancing for Television and Radio includes:

- Practical advice on how to make a start; where to find work; writing the right kind of CV, networking and making contacts
- An important section on maintaining and developing a freelance career as well as a chapter on the challenges and responsibilities of setting up and running a small business.
- A significant chapter on the basics of writing and submitting programme proposals to broadcasters as well as a substantial section of useful contact information.

ISBN 10: 0–415–34101–9 (hbk)
ISBN 10: 0–415–34102–7 (pbk)

ISBN 13: 9–78–0–415–34101–1 (hbk)
ISBN 13: 9–78–0–415–34102–8 (pbk)

Available at all good bookshops
For ordering and further information please visit:
www.routledge.com